Our Time is Now.

Notes from the high school underground.

Our Time is Now.

Notes from the high school underground.

EDITOR
JOHN BIRMINGHAM

INTRODUCTION
KURT VONNEGUT, JR.

PRAEGER PUBLISHERS
NEW YORK • WASHINGTON • LONDON

PRAEGER PUBLISHERS
111 FOURTH AVENUE, NEW YORK, N.Y. 10003, U.S.A.
5, CROMWELL PLACE, LONDON S.W.7, ENGLAND

PUBLISHED IN THE UNITED STATES OF AMERICA IN 1970
BY PRAEGER PUBLISHERS, INC.

SECOND PRINTING, 1970

LIBRARY OF CONGRESS CATALOG CARD
NUMBER: 77–99813

PRINTED IN THE UNITED STATES OF AMERICA

DESIGN BY UNA McGEEHAN
FIST SYMBOL BY TODD ASH

Contents

v

Introduction
by KURT VONNEGUT, JR.

I went to Shortridge High School in Indianapolis, Indiana. It was and still is one of the few American high schools with a daily paper. It was fashionable to write. Everybody was crazy about writing, and I'm writing still. So is Dan Wakefield, and so are a lot of other people who went there. It is such an old paper that my mother used to be on its staff, God rest her soul. Its name is the *Echo*, which is an honest name for an officially sanctioned student paper. Everything I said in it echoed off the grownups around me, which was all right with me back then. Thinking back, I am not persuaded that I was a complete fool to be content with echoing. I admired a lot of my teachers—still do. Many of them are still teaching, and I pay them calls from time to time.

One thing that was lucky for me: My high school years were from 1936 into 1940, and the Great Depression was still pretty mean, and the smartest people in town had turned to teaching. I don't think the smartest people do that any more. Times change.

The poet of my graduating class had this to say in the front of our yearbook, which, incidentally, celebrated the seventy-fifth anniversary of the school:

> Where go the years?
> But moments fleet, uncertain,
> That swiftly speed and disappear
> From mortal view?

Where go the years?
To seek the darkness and to hide
Within the dust of old hall clocks?
Or ride forgotten moonbeams
To the sky?

I don't laugh or even smile at that high school poem now. Where *do* go the years? That's an excellent guess—that they ride forgotten moonbeams to the sky. The author was Phyllis Heidenreich.

Phyllis—where are you now?

I will tell you where a lot of our classmates are: They're in soldiers' graves. When I go back to Indianapolis, I sometimes stand beneath the great bronze casualty lists which are bolted to the walls in the entrance hall of Shortridge, and I read all the names, and I marvel silently, "My God—so that's what became of him . . . and him . . . and him . . . and him." It's easy for me to imagine that all those dead young men are lawyers and realtors and insurance salesmen and teachers and engineers and so on. But they're not.

I reread those casualty lists again very recently, made old friends and enemies stop mowing lawns and barbecuing steaks in my imagination, made them climb back into their graves. And then I went downtown to a television station to promote a new book of mine. It was a pacifistic book. One of my television co-stars was the man in charge of the Indianapolis 500-mile Speedway Parade. Another was "Little Richard," a black rock musician who had given the Beatles their start in international show business. He took them to Germany with him.

Little Richard was wearing an electric blue dashiki, and he would periodically shout, even while the parade marshal or I was speaking, "Let it all hang out!" So I did let it all hang out. I expressed my disgust at the

Viet Nam War, said I had four sons of military age, that none of them was going, because it was an unjust war, and so on.

The next day, I heard that a beloved relative of mine was going around town saying he was shocked by my lack of patriotism. Well, he shouldn't have been. I was exhibiting the sort of patriotism that used to be taught, during the Great Depression, by the best teachers in the Indianapolis public schools. We were proud back then of our tiny standing army, proud of our civilian wisdom in keeping the military in its place. We were horrified by war.

Times change.

So I've taken this space in the front of John Birmingham's good book to record something which I've wanted to record somewhere for a long time, something easily forgotten: My generation was raised to be pacifistic, but it fought well in a war it felt was just. This is surely true of the pacifists in the present high school generation: They aren't cowards, either.

And much of what they object to in contemporary society came into being during World War II. That was when warlike thinking and Prussian attitudes toward unquestioning obedience became so popular. Too bad.

I wrote a piece for *The New York Times* not long ago, which contained some reflections on high school as it used to be. In it, I was amazed that a girl I had gone to school with was now Mrs. Melvin Laird, the wife of our Secretary of Defense. I quoted an Indianapolis friend on that subject:

> When you get to be our age, you all of a sudden realize that you are being ruled by people you went to high school with. You all of a sudden catch on that life is nothing *but* high school. You make a fool of yourself in

high school, then you go to college to learn how you should have acted in high school, then you get out into real life, and that turns out to be high school all over again—class officers, cheerleaders, and all.

He was right.

High school is closer to the core of the American experience than anything else I can think of, which is why this book is so full of shocks of recognition for Americans in almost any walk of life. We have all been there. While there, we saw nearly every form of justice and injustice, kindness and meanness, intelligence and stupidity which we were likely to encounter in later life.

Richard Nixon is a familiar type from high school. So is Melvin Laird. So is J. Edgar Hoover. So is General Lewis Hershey. So is everybody.

Consequently—the mere striplings who have contributed to this book are dealing with issues to which few Americans can remain indifferent, since they are the main issues of life itself. And I am bound to say that the striplings discuss life as it is and as it should be as intelligently as did the authors of the *Federalist Papers*. They tell us not only what seems wrong to them but what can be done to make things better. What could be more decent and hopeful than that?

The words in this book do not come from the mouths of babes. They come from the mouths of adults in high school. As to the people who tell these young adults that they must not speak as frankly as they do, because the officially adult community will be outraged: They are right in a way, but that way is cowardly.

This is the home of the brave. Remember?

Editor's Foreword

I decided from the beginning that this book would be written entirely by high school students and people who, like myself, just graduated. (In most cases, even the students who just graduated wrote the articles while they were still in high school.) It isn't that I don't like writers over eighteen or that I don't believe that anyone over eighteen could have any important ideas about the high school underground. I just think that it is important that the students tell the story from their point of view for once. *The New York Times* has printed some very nice articles about underground papers in New York City, but they (and the rest of the media) have yet to really show it from the students' point of view.

I cannot claim this book completely for myself; it belongs to the high school underground. So I want to begin by thanking all the students and underground papers who helped me to get this book into existence. I especially thank: *Mine*, Tucson, Arizona; *Freethinker*, La Puente, California; Adelaide, Pacific Grove, California; *T.R.I.P.*, Long Beach, California; *Cornucopia*, *Jugendbewegung*, and *Oink!*, Downey, California; *The Nickel Bag*, Westport, Connecticut; *The Pearl Before the Swine*, Clearwater, Florida; Karen Lewis, Pecos, Texas; *Homesick Blue*, Corpus Christi, Texas; *Trash-burner*, Monroe, Washington; *Links*, Madison, Wisconsin; *Diogenes' Lantern*, Waitsburg, Washington;

Doormat Dwellers, Woodville, Wisconsin; *The Open Door*, Milwaukee, Wisconsin; *In-Between*, Hamilton, Ohio; Ross McConnell, Columbus, Ohio; *The Messiah*, Lombardi, Illinois; *Minstrel*, Waukegan, Illinois; *Common Sense*, Alton, Illinois; *The American Revelation*, Elgin, Illinois; *The Green Groad*, Topeka, Kansas; *Finger*, Gretna, Louisiana; *Insight*, Britton, Michigan; *Omega*, Royal Oak, Michigan; Jerry Weis, Morris Plains, New Jersey; *Mindfood*, Pelham, New York; *Frox*, Long Beach, New York; *John Bowne Was a Pacifist*, Flushing, New York; *Interobang*, Mamaroneck, New York; *Weakly Reader*, *New York Herald Tribune*, *High School Free Press*, *Enragé*, and, especially, Honest Bob Singer and Toby Mamis, New York, New York; *The Virgin*, Upper Saddle River, New Jersey; and the *Oracle* and Gail Christie, Mahwah, New Jersey; etc., etc.

JOHN BIRMINGHAM

P.S. Thanks to Kenne Solomon for the title.

Our Time is NOW.

Notes from the high school underground.

A *generation gap.* The one you hear about most is the gap between the over-thirty and the under-thirty. I'm seventeen, so I am supposed to say that if you are over thirty you are against me, and if you are under thirty you are with me.

Besides calling it cliché, I could criticize anyone

ONE   Discovering the Underground

---

who uses the term "gap," because it means putting people into groups—boxes. But I won't. I know enough to see that you can't get by as a human without putting people into boxes. My real objection to the way people talk about the gap is that they have made only two age-group boxes—the over-thirty and the under-thirty. If you are going to put people into boxes, the least you can do is give them a wide variety of boxes to fit into.

A generation gap is the result of what has happened during the twenty years that lie between two generations. During this time, the younger generation has been forming a new culture, new politics, and new means of communicating with each other. At the same time, the older generation has been holding onto the culture, politics, and media that were developed twenty years ago. The more that times have changed during these twenty years, the more difference has developed between the generations.

Today the younger generation is typified in the eyes of most adults by the college revolutionaries. What does the younger generation do? They take over college buildings. That is the stereotype you are supposed to fit. But another—different—revolutionary movement has begun to erupt in the high schools. Of course, this movement does not get as much coverage by the over-thirty media because it is presently on a smaller scale than the college-campus rebellions. And the people involved in media generally put the high school revolutionaries into the same box as the college revolutionaries. This stereotype has to be dealt with before we can discuss the high school underground fairly.

The easiest way is to create a couple of new age-group boxes and point out a gap that is virtually unheard of— the gap between high school and college students.

Times change so fast that three years now can form a gap that might be equal to a gap formed by twenty years in the last century. College students—mostly the Students for a Democratic Society (SDS)—don't fully understand why they were unable to organize the high schools. In a way, they were ignoring the gap. Often they like to think of themselves as fathers to the high school underground, but, in reality, college revolutionaries play only a small part in the evolution of the high school revolution. Yes, a lot of high school SDS groups have been formed, in California and Washington especially, but these groups usually act on their own, without college-student influence. And high school SDS's are not as common as totally independent high school underground movements.

Last summer, the SDS sent out a newsletter that was directed to high school revolutionaries, urging them to start underground papers. This might seem to indicate that the SDS was partially responsible for organizing the high school students. But the opposite is true. This newsletter was only repeating what high school students had already said many times. And it was urging high school students to do what they were already doing—completely on their own. In fact, many high school revolutionaries whom I have spoken to talk of SDSers as though they are "over the hill." These high school students (myself included) believe that their own movement is far more important than the college movement. They believe that it is more important because it includes all youth. High school is responsible at one time or another for the education of all young people in America.

At seventeen, I am younger than some people and older than others. Things change fast enough in our society so that seventeen is not like twenty-one, nor is it like fifteen. I may not have as much experience in organizing students for a political revolution as some SDSers have, but, by the same token, I have not made their mistakes—destructive mistakes, such as trying to cause change through violence and violation of other students' rights. At the same time, I should not be lumped together with students much younger than me. Just because we both put out underground papers in our schools, I don't think I should be put into the same box as Joshua Mamis, who helped to put out a junior high school underground paper at the age of twelve.

And now that I have graduated, I will be going to college. This won't mean that I will be changing from one movement to another. That isn't what it will mean for most high school revolutionaries who go to college. Instead of joining the college movement as it exists today, they will change it into a new movement that will begin tomorrow. Joshua Mamis and others like him will then be changing the high schools.

Today the high school revolutionaries are looking for *really* new ideas. They won't just settle for standard proposals that have been handed to them by the SDS or some radical adults. Norman Mailer discovered this when he went to a meeting of students in the high school underground in New York during his campaign for the Democratic mayoral nomination. A girl there told him that he sounded just like her parents.

Probably the best way of destroying the stereotype is to let the high school underground speak for itself in all its variety of voices. Maybe only 5 per cent of high school students are actively involved in the underground movement, but that 5 per cent is enough to lead, to cause some change in the high schools, and to cater to the needs of high school students in a way that teachers and administrators never could.

The revolution began for me personally in May, 1969—in the form of a crudely printed underground magazine called *Smuff*. Inside were eleven pages on the war in Vietnam, student radicalism, draft-dodging, and Hackensack High School. I was the editor-in-chief out of *necessity*. And I soon discovered that what was happening in Hackensack was also happening all over the high school scene, south as well as north, west as well as east. Out of *necessity*—everywhere.

What *necessity* was it that created an underground so vigorously that we can now justifiably talk of a revolution of our own?

Take my case. It's no exception.

I began my senior year in high school as editor-in-chief of the *Voice*, Hackensack High School's official overground newspaper. The staff and I were able to change and improve the format of the paper a lot, but we made little immediate change in the content. The first article that aroused any controversy was an open letter to students about interracial dating. The letter was not especially radical or shocking, yet our principal told us that it could not be printed in the *Voice* because it would arouse too much controversy. He also said that he was skeptical because the letter was anonymous.

After several discussions, and a lengthy letter from the *Voice* faculty advisor against this censorship, the principal allowed us to print the letter.

Although it seemed that we had won this battle, it was really just the first battle of a war. Each issue of the *Voice* after that had something in it that the principal objected to. In the next two issues, we were refused permission to print an advertisement for draft counseling, and part of an editorial about a cut in the proposed school budget.

My biggest problem with censorship, though, was that I had to fight for articles that I didn't even care about. The students who wrote the really controversial and thought-provoking articles would not write for the *Voice*, because they assumed that anything that they had to say would be censored. So I was left fighting to get a draft-counseling ad printed when I should have been fighting for articles by students who I thought would make the *Voice* a more relevant newspaper.

Just how widespread is the problem of censorship became evident to me at a Columbia Scholastic Press Association convention in February, 1969. During this convention, attended by representatives of hundreds of high school overground newspapers like the *Voice*, several student-run meetings were held to discuss the problem of censorship. The first meeting I went to was so crowded that a few dozen students—including me—had to sit on the floor. Students spent most of the time complaining about the administration at their school and its attitude toward censorship. My reaction was one of relief and disgust that I was not alone in my censorship problems. However, few of the speakers offered any solutions.

In fact, the only student who gave a real solution was the organizer of the meeting. He urged all students who had this problem to quit their position on their overground paper and go underground. He was confident that any student who really wanted to express his opinion could do it, whether the administration liked it or not. I thought he was right, but still I continued to work on the Voice.

Back in Hackensack, two juniors, Jay Dunkelman and Edd Luwish, planned to start an underground paper, Smuff, and so I suggested that they try to get their articles into the Voice. They responded simply by showing me the articles and asking me if the administration would let them be published. I doubted it. Soon the Voice was censored again and Smuff was not yet out. Luwish and Dunkelman asked a senior, Bob Cohen, and me to help to hurry it into existence. Since the situation of the Voice had not improved, I accepted the job as editor.

While I was working for Smuff, I continued editing the Voice, and, in a last attempt to change his mind about censorship, I sent a letter to the principal. He read it, but the letter did not get the results I had hoped for. So I reprinted the letter in Smuff so the whole school could read it:

> I am sure that you are tired of hearing about censorship of the Voice. Nevertheless, I have more to say. We have discussed, although not with each other, all the standard arguments for and against censorship in general. And nothing has been resolved. For that reason, I will try to be specific and synthesize the Voice censorship issue into one question. The question is: Can you safely give your responsibility and authority as censor to the students on the Editorial Board of the Voice? You have already said that you do not want to give up your authority as censor because you are ultimately responsible for everything that comes out of this school. Your position is easily defensible. You will be taking a risk if you give authority to the students. But isn't giving authority to students part of educating them? And isn't taking risks part of being an educator? I think that the good that would result from your giving the power of censorship

to students would outweigh the risk. To illustrate my point of view, I have chosen a paragraph from a letter that was written by Hubert H. Humphrey to Mr. Napoleon Jean Papale. The letter appeared in the 1969 Yearbook for the New Jersey Secondary Teachers' Association:

> One of the answers it seems to me is give our young more authority—the kind of authority that generates responsibility—in the academic society which forms such an important part of their lives. A great many of them can handle additional authority well; and if we trust them now, I am convinced that we shall have a better, more trustworthy leadership in the future.

I am sure that you will consider my point of view with an open mind, as I have tried to consider yours. If you would like to discuss this subject with me further, I will gladly make myself available any day before school or during period five. However, I realize that you have a very busy schedule. I thank you for your time and await your reply.

I said in the letter that my principal's position was "defensible," and I meant it. I realized that he had to deal with parents who might become angry if the Voice was too controversial. To this extent, the school was a reflection of the adult world outside. Yet obviously it shouldn't be. It should be a healthy community of its own. If the administration worried more about students who might become angry if the Voice remained censored, instead of worrying about what parents might think, then student dissent would be less likely. I agree with the administration that a school has a responsibility to its community. But in school, the community consists of students and teachers, not parents. Parents, however, have the power—the power to vote on referendums and the power to get administrators fired if complaints are strong enough. The parents are the taxpayers. In many cases, too many cases, they see their children as part of their property. They believe they should control the way in which their property is treated in school.

It follows, therefore, that to get more freedom within the school so that it can cater to the needs of *their* time, not their parents', students must obtain some power of their own. Power means influence. They can't have the taxpaying power of their parents, they can't have teacher power, and so they must find their own. In my case, this meant fighting for the power of freedom of speech. The *Voice* had no real power, so perhaps we could find it in *Smuff*.

The first problem was money. An underground paper is much more difficult to get out than an overground paper, simply because the students cannot use the school building and do not have the support of the teachers or administrator: They have to make it entirely on their own. First, we found the printing process that was cheapest for us. *Smuff* publisher Bob Cohen suggested that we use his father's blueprint machine. So our only cost was paper, but that was expensive enough—$150 for what we needed. (A blueprint machine uses chemically treated paper that is yellow on one side.) To raise money, we got about twenty-five students and one teacher (who is more like a student) to contribute $2.50, $5.00, or $10.00. We promised that on the following Monday they would receive their money's worth of *Smuff* at 15 cents a copy. Most students were reluctant (remember, any revolution is a minority thing), but we were able to raise the money.

Meanwhile, we worked fast to collect enough articles. I did an interview with my sister about "What Last Year's Valedictorian *Really* Thinks about H.H.S." Another student had written a letter to New Jersey Senator Case about the legalization of marijuana, and since the senator had responded to his letter, we printed both letters side-by-side. (It's a good idea to have a contribution from a senator in your underground newspaper.) Other pages were filled with student opinion and student poetry.

Bob Cohen tried to advertise *Smuff* the Friday before *Smuff* came out. He cut a stencil for a duplicator to make a leaflet, but he made the mistake of trying to use a school machine. He was caught and sent to the principal. The principal, who had already heard of *Smuff*, reprimanded Bob and said that he should not distribute *Smuff* in school.

This worried us, so we called the local American Civil Liberties Union. The man I talked to was encouraging and said that we should go ahead with our plans. He said that if we were suspended, he would have ACLU lawyers working for us as soon as we called.

It was Friday evening, so with that worry over, we began to type up the *Smuff* that I had already cited. We found blueprinting 11,000 pages was long, tedious labor, even if you came at it with revolutionary zeal. The original pages must be typed up as neatly as possible on onionskin paper. Then each page must be printed by placing the original copy over the yellow side of the blueprint and putting them through the first process to expose the blueprint paper to light. The paper becomes white except for the parts that have been hidden from the light by the typewriting. The two papers are then separated and the blueprint paper is sent through an ammonia process that causes any yellow part of the paper to turn dark blue. Doing this 11,000 times is insane.

Friday night we blueprinted with only three people: Bob, Russ Fisher, and me. Bob got about two hours sleep that night, but Russ and I slept late on Saturday morning.

Saturday night we got help. Altogether, about nine people were working there that night. We got a system worked out for printing and collating. By ten o'clock the next morning, we had printed, collated, and stapled almost 1,000 copies, 11 pages each. That evening, Bob and a couple of other students drove to each of the distributors' homes and gave them envelopes of *Smuff*. The envelopes were marked "Please do not disrupt. Do not sell copies in classrooms without permission."

Monday, the school was flooded with *Smuff*. Our distribution was very successful. Everyone in the school seemed to have read it—someone else's copy if not their own. Teachers seemed even more eager to buy than students. We sold out (about 1,000 copies in a school of more than 2,000 students). We received a lot of criticism, destructive and constructive, but generally the reaction was favorable. Many teachers spent class periods discussing the right of students to put it out. As one student said in a letter to the editor that appeared in the second issue, we had "made a fairly loud noise inside these musty, crumby walls of H.H.S."

I had to commend the administration. Contrary to what I had expected, they responded to *Smuff* by "turning their backs." It was what I would have done in their place.

We followed the first issue with another in about three weeks. It was easier to collect material this time, since many students now wanted to take advantage of their new, uncensored voice. The second issue was slicker and more professional than the first. We abandoned the blueprint machine and had it printed by professional offset. The second issue did not make as loud a noise, because it was not a new thing, but we sold more copies of it than we did of the first issue.

With the second issue, we started the *Smuff* Student Coalition, an underground union designed to represent the students where our student council had failed. Since we were trying to organize a maximum number of students, and since we had lots of *Smuff* left over (we had printed 1,500 copies this time), we decided to go to Teaneck, a nearby high school, to sell *Smuff*. Bob Cohen printed a flyer for Teaneck and went to the school the next day to distribute *Smuff* outside the building. We didn't do much business, however, because we discovered we weren't exactly bringing our revolutionary message to virgin territory. The day before, Teaneck students had come out with not one but two underground papers simultaneously. It was our first heady realization that we were not alone in our underground activities in New Jersey. However, having made the selling trip, Bob and another Hackensack student, Milton Galfas, decided to go and see if there was any business inside. Simply stated, they were caught, brought back to Hackensack, and got into trouble. They were not, however, punished as severely as they might have been. One teacher told Bob, for example, that if he had been an administrator, he would have expelled him.

The trouble that resulted from distributing in Teaneck was enlightening, in that it gave us an insight into our opposition. While the reaction to the first issue seemed to have been favorable from most of the faculty, there was still a faction of teachers who had not been heard from. When we were caught distributing in Teaneck, we provoked many teachers who had been in silent opposition to *Smuff* into expressing their opinions loudly. According to one teacher who supported *Smuff*, "suspend the staff of *Smuff*" was the talk of the faculty lounge.

These reactions to *Smuff* also gave us more reason to continue publication of *Smuff*. Up until that time, we had not been sure of why we were going to all that trouble—with the risk of much more trouble. Bob Cohen did it mostly for the experience. He enjoyed doing projects outside of school and he realized that he learned more from these projects than he did from school. I did it partly because of my trouble with censorship and partly for the experience. Putting out *Smuff* made the end of my senior year go faster than it would have otherwise. The reactions to *Smuff* also kept us going. Of course, the students and teachers who valued it were reasons to keep on publishing. But even the people who hated it gave us a reason to continue. The people who hated *Smuff* most seemed to read it most carefully. They read it more carefully than they ever read the *Voice*. And *Smuff* was more successful at arousing students than any cheerleader that . year. I don't think our backgrounds influenced us much. Our sheer diversity was expressed well, I thought, at one of our meetings. Don Carlo asked me why Nick Dunn, our "token Negro," wasn't at the meeting. We all pointed out to him that our "token Negro" might not be there, but our "token Jew" was, and our "token Irish Catholic" (me), our "token White Anglo-Saxon Protestant," and our "token female." It was a thoroughly "token" meeting. But one thing that everyone present had in common was a desire to see a revolutionary change in the school system. And after our experience at Teaneck—with its *two* underground papers—we knew that we weren't alone in our county but were really part of a movement.

Before the second issue of *Smuff* came out, a teacher showed me a copy of the *New York High School Free Press*; I decided to go to its office to interview someone there for *Smuff* and try to learn more about the high school underground at other schools. When I got there, I discovered that the apartment in which it was located also acted as the offices for the High School Independent Press Service (HIPS), a national press service, and the High School Student Union. It was also a commune that housed about a dozen high school students. Everyone in the commune was polite to me, and they gave me my interview without hesitation.

What I learned astonished me. *Smuff*—or its equivalent—had broken out all over.

ROBBY NEWTON (by courtesy of *Smuff*, Vol. I, No 2):
All year the Student Union has been slowly developing
the *High School Free Press*. The Student Union mostly
came out of a radical, anti-imperialist, anti-capitalist
movement, starting with a student mobilization committee. Then over last summer, it tried to gear its
programs to the high schools. We'd been organizing
in the high schools for two years already—there was a
small group of people who'd been around that long—
but we had never related our programs to the schools
that much. You know, we had been talking about "stop
imperialism; stop aggression," but they were just words.
So we went into the schools to talk about the schools.
And it started out with some very Mickey Mouse stuff.
You know, about dress codes—for guys wearing long hair
and girls to wear pants. From there we quickly got
into free speech stuff. Because no matter where you
start in the high schools, you have to get into free
speech, because they don't let you say anything. They
won't let you give out papers . . . In the beginning
it was all very exciting. We were a new thing—it started
with 300 kids at the founding convention. And then we
were all big for the revolution. But in a month or two it
started to really fumble. And then the teachers' strike
started. It was really strange because before that, the
only issues that we dealt with were really Mickey
Mouse. And here the teachers' strike was really heavy
stuff. It affected hundreds of thousands of people and
we related to it. Of course we were against the strike
because it was racist. So during the strike, the Student
Union went around opening up schools. Parent groups
and the Board of Ed did that, too, but they couldn't
keep the schools open. You know, they couldn't do

it very heavily because the parents had to work, and the Board of Ed couldn't do shit. But when we opened a school, we could put kids into it and actually run it. So we did that and we gained momentum. Soon, we had most of the high schools open with kids going to them every day. And the kids who were going who were Student Union kids—or ASA (Afro-American Student Association) or BSU (Black Students' Union) kids—were pushing not only to have the schools open, but to run them themselves as well. And from there we got into this student power thing. We are supporting community control and community control in the high schools *is* student power. We believe that high school students are legitimately adult. They shouldn't have to bother with parents; they should be allowed to control their school. So the teachers' strike ended. And the agreement was that there would be an extra forty-five minutes added on to each day—five minutes on each period. All this so that the UFT teachers could get equal pay. It was really bad. A teacher who had struck for ten weeks and then taught for the rest of the year actually made a profit between the strike benefits and the extra time. The teachers were to be paid time and a half for overtime on the extra five minutes at the end of each period they worked. As it turned out, most teachers only worked for five periods yet they were paid for nine. Holidays like Christmas week and Thanksgiving weekend were school days. So then there were riots. On the Friday after Thanksgiving that was ordinarily a holiday, there were riots in high schools all over the city. And the same things happened on Monday and Tuesday. And then on Wednesday there was a raid. Most of these riots had been spontaneous. Then over the next few weeks there was a lot of building alliances with the black groups. And then, suddenly, it all stopped. Through January, February, and the first half of March, everything was stagnating. The only

16 OUR TIME IS NOW

things that happened during that period was that the *Free Press* and the HIPS packets got out. No one knew what to do. So we started to look for something to do, like some programs. And we were really grasping at straws. Like we signed one program that all of us disagreed with, and even then we questioned it. It was an anti-militarist program. Some Columbia SDS people wrote up a high school version of their program. It was really rhetorical. It talked about anti-militarism as a major issue in the high schools, which it's not. For high school kids who get into the army, the army is getting away from home and away from lousy jobs and it's maybe learning a skill. When the army is the best alternative for some kids, you shouldn't say, "But the army is imperialist and capitalist." But during this period we were looking for just any program that came up. It was really weird. But the March tenth issue of the *Free Press* was a real turning point. I mean we got some really good stuff. Like we got this report of the New York High School Principals' Association Committee on student unrest. And we got it illegally. So we had that in the next issue of the *Free Press*. And that issue was also an important issue because it was like the first time that the Student Union's program really became part of the *Free Press* and vice-versa. Like we had the spring offensive laid out which was really written by the Student Union.

ME: Do you get busted for distributing the *Free Press* in schools?

ROBBY: Well, we never get arrested, but everyone gets suspended. I mean I haven't been suspended because I don't do that much work in the school. I'm too involved in the commune shit. But the kids who distribute get suspended for distributing unauthorized literature. We also got blamed for everything by the New York newspapers. Like the *Times* and the *News* kept saying that we were responsible for all disorders. Because the two weeks after April twenty-first, there were demonstrations and riots in every high school. One article in the *Post* called for conspiracy charges against us. So we printed the names of every reporter who wrote about it as the staff of *Free Press*.

ME: What kind of power does the Student Union have? Does it have any power with the administration? Can you act in the schools?

ROBBY: No . . .

ME: How much student support do you have?

ROBBY: That depends on what you mean by support. We don't measure things in those terms. Like now we are trying to do things with five or ten kids in every high school—five or ten kids is a lot. You can do things with five or ten. It wouldn't be hard for us to close any school down. If we do a little work and put out a leaflet, there's a strike. There's no problem. Right now there are like 200 people around the city that identify with the Student Union. That's just to give you an idea. Yet those few hundred can close the schools down, if we wanted to. There's a really small group of people who are real organizers. So we in this office— which is a commune, too—relate to those people. We know what moves people, like what programs, and we apply these programs with our tools. Like the *Free Press* is a tremendous tool. It helped bring a lot of people together and it generated a lot of energy.

ME: Does the SDS ever come into your schools?

JAIME FRIAR: Yes, they cause big hassles. The SDS has really fucked up politics.

ROBBY: Now they're really hung up on trying to organize the working class.

JAIME: They can't. They tried to organize the high school students and failed. Remember when that guy came to our school? What's his name?

JIM GAMOR: Crudd.

JAIME: Yeah, Crudd. He was trying to make a deep

political speech to a bunch of high school kids who knew nothing about politics.

ROBBY: Soon we are going to the NC [a national meeting for SDS] to tell them how fucked they are. We are going to tell them to decentralize.

ME: What is the main program for the *Free Press* and the Student Union now?

ROBBY: It is being centered around taking back youth culture. Something about youth culture is revolutionary. It started on the streets. Grateful Dead and the Airplane started playing on the streets. And now this all has been taken over by big groups like Columbia Records. All these fucking capitalists have taken over our culture. So we're going to take it back. We will demand that all rock groups play for free in places like Sheep Meadow where 35,000 people can listen. And all profits should be turned back to the youth culture for things like rock groups and motorcycle gangs. But we know that we can't really get these things. Our purpose is to educate. We will show the kids what they've got. Because if they become aware of it they can hold on to it.

ME: Then do you think that students can learn more by working with things like the Student Union and the *Free Press* than they do in classes and in school?

ROBBY: Obviously, why do you ask?

ME: Well, this is supposed to be an interview, so I am supposed to get you to say things like that instead of saying them myself.

ROBBY: O.K.

O.K. . . . What that interview told me clearly was that the high school underground movement was on a larger scale than I'd ever imagined. I realized that we were just in the first stages in my school. The high school students in the New York City underground talked about a movement that had had time to develop, a movement that had already been involved in riots as well as in producing underground papers. One of the most meaningful lessons I learned was that where it had had a chance to develop, the underground was dealing with issues that are more directly concerned with the schools than censorship. Student power, of course, was a big issue. The students simply wanted more control over the school of which they were part— as we did. I also understood that the underground movement was, or should be, deeply concerned with cultural revolution. As Robby Newton said, "Something about this youth culture is revolutionary." The culture was an essential part of the movement and, therefore, the movement should protect the culture. Youth culture was to be valued by the young and was worth fighting for. This should be one of our major aims. Also, through the underground press and any other "tools" we had, we should educate our fellow students about how and where the schools had failed us. Were failing us.

By the end of the school year, I was in touch with the editors of several high school underground papers, and these contacts soon led to others.

The editor of the *Oracle*, a nearby underground paper in Mahwah, New Jersey, telephoned me after reading about *Smuff* in a local county newspaper. She wanted

TWO How Far Should We Go?

to know how I got away with distributing *Smuff* on school grounds.

Soon afterward, I was also contacted by Honest Bob Singer, editor of the *Weakly Reader* (sic), of Stuyvesant High School in New York City. He had read an advertisement I had put in the *East Village Other* offering to buy high school underground papers.

In a few weeks, I obtained, through assorted grapevines and much help from the high school commune, the names and addresses of about 150 high school underground papers. I wrote to all of them.

The size of the response surprised me. In less than two weeks after I mailed out the letters, I had a collection of more than twenty-five different papers, often with several issues of each. I learned that despite HIPS, the National High School Press Service, students involved in the underground still craved for more communication. Letters often addressed me as "friend" or "brother" and urged me to continue the correspondence and exchange of papers. Everyone seemed anxious to tell me their story. I gathered that although the underground was spread through all fifty states (except *perhaps* Alaska—I didn't get any contacts there), the reasons for getting into it and how it developed often varied a great deal from state to state, from school to school.

One of the first letters I received—from Stuart Steffan, John B. Koskinen, and Richard Shadden, the three editors of the *Minstrel*, of Waukegan, Illinois—not only pointed out these differences inside the underground but argued that they were important for its success. After inviting *Smuff* to join them in a "semi-syndicate" —an example of *Minstrel* initiative!—they explained that their paper was at its lowest point when it was not their own work but was based simply on the material they obtained from HIPS.

Because their letter raises several important points about the development of the underground, I think I should let it speak for itself:

> . . . we did get into some trouble with the administration, but nothing in the way of them ordering that we no longer print and distribute, which was quite fortunate and completely unexpected. However, we did receive other threats. Threats in the form of threats against our person, crosses burned on lawns and on top of doghouses (really!) and threatening phone calls. We also received harassment from reactionary drivers, education teachers, and some students. Fortunately though, nothing that would ever demand or warrant our suspension of publication. . . .
>
> The first edition was very amateurish and the less said about that one the better. But being the only alternative to the crap that was printed in the student paper, "The Student 'W' World," it was still accepted warmly, but circulation and costs were a problem. Our circulation was not high enough to meet our costs.
>
> The first edition's emphasis was placed, unfortunately, too heavily on literature. As it turned out, the literature was not that good to begin with.

Despite fiscal problems, the second edition came out in about three weeks following the first. Financing was once again a problem. We thought we could remedy the situation by raising the price. Unfortunately, as is frequently the case, that didn't work either. Circulation fell as we grew more timid to push it, and the students more timid to buy it. Again you will find the emphasis on literature, rather than politics or anything else. The only politics came out of HIPS. Their articles were not much better written than were ours—worse, as a matter of fact.

In the third edition, we thought we had hit upon the solution to the problem of finances—subscriptions. And maintaining the high price and raising it in the future issues. After a disappointing record of four subscriptions and no increase in circulation, we abandoned the idea. The third edition was more political but everything was HIPS. We were no longer our own publication, but merely a soap box for HIPS. After review of their material and the typical crap that they gave us, we abandoned the idea of using anything else from HIPS, thereby enabling us to have better rapport with the students and the particular situation at our school.

The fourth edition did not come out for two months after the third. Everyone thought we had given up the ghost. Not actually, we just became engrossed in the student movement at our particular school. We spent much more time on that than on the paper. One of the articles in the fourth edition explains a little of the background. After much petty politics, policies and practices that were getting us, in general, and the movement in particular, nowhere, and the realization that, while we are very left-minded, we are not radicals (we do not believe in violent revolution and therefore are not qualified as radicals; no cause, no matter what it is, can justify the killing of another man; we and the paper have become quite pacifistic), we quit the student movement and returned to *Minstrel*.

After quitting the movement, and striking out on our own once again, we came out with another issue as soon as possible, the fourth edition. One can notice the change immediately. *Minstrel* had become worth reading. We abandoned the idea of selling it. We gave it away. We doubled circulation. Second and third hand circulation grew. Our message spread to many more students. For fiscal support we asked for and received many donations. We also asked for and received a few ads. We actually broke even on that edition. The content became balanced. The articles were worth reading, and we received compliments from students as well as a few teachers. Satire (decent satire) became another part of *Minstrel*. And one of our best. In that edition we were noted by the teachers for our essays; by the students, for our satire. . . .

Which brings us to the fifth edition. Undoubtedly the most controversial. We had become braver and braver as the year went along. We let out the stops on this edition. . . . This was the edition that brought about the harassment, crossburnings, threatening phone calls, and some conferences with the Administration. It was tremendous . . . "Oh, Please Jim!" is significant in several ways. First it gave a name to the student council (the students referred to it as the ding-aling dynasty for the remainder of the year, including members of student council). And second, that this article was a factor in the retirement of one student council sponsor and the resignation of another. Or so we were told by the student council treasurer. The recommendations for the improvement of student council were universally accepted by the students (including next year's president), but not by the administration. Circulation of the fifth edition was higher than that of the "Student 'W' World" (ours reached almost the entire student body at East campus of Waukegan High School, over 2,000, unlike the " 'W' World" which had a circulation of 1,000 at both campuses of Waukegan High School containing 4,000 students). It established us as the student paper. (We also brought about the extinction of the Radicals' underground paper, *Fresh Air*, with that edition.)

The next and last edition was calmer than the other

and not as controversial as the previous, with the exception of the satirical semester test at the end of that edition. We had restored what we felt was the proper balance of literature and politics. The circulation remained high. We received compliments from students who had threatened us before. You'll notice a goodly part of this edition is dealing with the letters we received and our response to them. Oh, yes, you are quite fortunate to receive this copy, it was the last one that we had. It is also missing the ads, so it is actually incomplete but we doubted whether you cared to see the ad. Circulation was that great. . . .

One final point of advice, it's free, so you can listen to it or ignore it. Never let yourself be influenced by, taken over by, or dominated by anyone other than yourself. You'll find that *Smuff* will be better for it.

All part of the underground, but all different. What, then, is the "underground"? For some it is more political than for others. As I use the word, it does not imply a degree of radicalism. A high school underground paper for me is just a paper that deals with a high school, but is produced outside the high school and is not authorized by the school authorities. Both the *Nickel Bag* and the *New York High School Free Press* are equally "underground," and yet they are very different.

Some papers aim at a restricted hip audience, some hope to reach a much wider readership. As an editor of *Hypo*, a paper in Camden, New Jersey, said to me, "Are you going to serve the hip community exclusively, or are you going to try to inform (and thus convert) the rednecks?" While I do not consider the people of Hackensack to be "rednecks," *Smuff*'s purpose to me was to serve the community of Hackensack High School, not just a group of hip students. Putting out a paper that would serve only Hackensack's hip community would not be worthwhile, since the hip community in Hackensack is relatively small.

In places where a large hip community exists, however, such a paper *is* worthwhile. In New York City, the *High School Free Press* serves the hip high school community almost exclusively. The *Free Press* makes little or no effort to communicate to adults, teachers, or conservative students. It is filled with four-letter words that put off most adults immediately, and its politics are militant.

When the staff of a paper decides whom they want to address, they sometimes say that they are deciding how "underground" they intend to be. The editor of the *Nickel Bag* in Georgetown, Connecticut, told me that the *Nickel Bag* was not as "underground" as *Smuff*. I disagreed, but it was really just a matter of semantics.

Many papers differ in their attitude toward violence and come up with different answers to such questions as: Can a genuine revolution ever occur without violence? Did Chicago prove that violence is the only alternative to oppression? The editors of the *Minstrel* seemed to feel that they weren't really radicals because they didn't believe in violent revolution. And while most of the high school underground does not call for violence, I have seen several papers and leaflets that have violence as a central theme. One leaflet I remember in particular was sent to me by the minister of propaganda for the United Liberation Front located in Morris Plains, New Jersey. Its last sentence was "The ground you are standing on is liberated zone; defend it!" The same student also sent me a filled-in coupon for the *Smuff* Student Coalition, which stated that we would accomplish our goals by peaceful means. At the bottom he had written: "Peaceful means?"

I'd answer that with another question: What can you achieve worthwhile through violence that can't be accomplished some other way? In the schools I know where violence has erupted, none of the results seemed to take us one step foward. In almost all cases, the violence scares the administration and hardens its opposition and the *status quo*. In some cases, school property is damaged. And in cases like the New York City riots to protest the loss of holidays that resulted from the teachers' strike, the schools end up with police roaming the school corridors. Too often, violence is used just for kicks. And too often it just gives adults something to point their finger at so they can write off the rest of the underground's actions and arguments. Sometimes the underground owes its start to a protest against *adult* violence. *John Bowne Was a Pacifist*, of Flushing, New York, for example, started as a protest paper against the war in Vietnam. It publicized peace marches for the Fifth Avenue Peace Parade Committee but later concentrated more on the activities in its own community at John Bowne High School. Yet many adults who object to any hint of youthful violence also oppose such direct expressions of pacifism. Adults sometimes seem very confused, unable to reflect a consistent philosophy all the way down the line. This sometimes drives the underground to extremes and also explains its continual emphasis on frankness, even four-letter frankness.

Some student radicals in the underground think the idea of action through papers too literary and indirect, and prefer the confrontations possible through demonstrations. In fact, in my county, demonstrations have been even more numerous than papers. I may be a literary type and therefore may be prejudiced, but I don't regard demonstrations as a true underground activity. They are a kind of statement, a statement that is made "overground" to the administration. They can be fun, and sometimes (depending on the type of demonstration), they can get you out of class, but they are also easier than putting out an underground paper, and they provide an illusion of power rather than power itself. One school I know demonstrated against censorship of its "overground" paper. The demonstrations may have opened the eyes of the administration a little wider, but censorship remained. However, if these same students had gone underground, they would have satisfied their need for freedom of speech and also demonstrated their power.

Although *Smuff* gave the students of Hackensack High School freedom of the press, I still felt that one of *Smuff*'s goals was to become "overground." In *Smuff* underground, students could say anything they wanted to say. I thought, however, that if it were an authorized publication of the school, the students' voices would be heard more loudly and what they had to say would be taken more seriously.

Now I doubt this. I think that something would be lost if the underground papers became overground. Maybe the reason is that part of the excitement would no longer be there. The administration would always know when the paper was going to come out. And even if they didn't censor the paper, they would probably know what was going to be in it. And as for how loudly the students' voices would be heard, the administration seems to read a paper more carefully when it is not authorized—partly because they must decide what to do about it. Paradoxically, some of the best things about the underground papers result from the fact that administrations are trying to suppress them.

Still, if the administration were to offer *Smuff* a position as an uncensored, authorized magazine for the students, I would gladly accept. This gesture from the administration would be a real sign of their desire to communicate with the students. Anyhow, this is not something that we will have to think about, because it is very unlikely that it will happen.

Where it has happened, it has not been successful. *Frox*, of Long Beach, New York, made an agreement with the administration so that it could be overground.

But the agreement failed. The following article from the first underground issue of *Frox* explains why, from *Frox*'s point of view.

EMERGENCY UNDERGROUND ISSUE

FROX
Vol. II, No. 3
Long Beach, N.Y.

Frox has been forced underground. After trying to play the game with the administration, we have finally realized that the cards are stacked against us.

Here's the story: Several months ago the *Frox* staff accepted a compromise with the administration allowing us to distribute in school, in accord with the American Civil Liberties Union statement on student publications. By doing so we agreed to submit articles to a faculty adviser for approval. Dr. [X———] was our faculty adviser, and refused to trust the matter with any other faculty member. All articles for the last issue had been submitted and approved. Two days before the publication date, we received a *music* article. In the hectic atmosphere of getting out a paper, we unfortunately neglected to show Dr. [X———] this article. The article was straightforward and did not violate any of our agreement by being inflammatory, libelous or obscene. Dr. [X———] was furious and immediately suspended distribution (we only managed to get out half our papers). Although we realize we were at fault, we feel that Dr. [X———]'s two-month suspension of distribution was totally excessive, and an attempt to screw us.

The school board claims, "It is the aim of our high school to encourage students to freely express themselves, in writing or otherwise, as part of their educational program." These are strong words presented clearly, without ambiguity. Yet they are only *words:* empty and insincere. When the administration saw that we were planning a court case, they decided to compromise and allow us to distribute—under their conditions; conditions which led to their downfall, that being their control over us.

We can no longer be driven into a corner. We must be free. *Viva la causa!*

The administration at Long Beach High School is considered by many to be "liberal." But the *Frox* incident showed that even most "liberal" administrations aren't yet ready to give students more freedom of expression without a watchful eye (a possible censor's eye) being kept on them. They aren't completely trusted and therefore find it hard to trust in return.

There have been more successful agreements where the administration hasn't insisted on such tight control over what appears. *Interobang,* of Mamaroneck, N.Y.; *Albatross,* of Jacksonville, Illinois; and the *Searcher,* of Wellesley, Massachusetts, all received permission to distribute on school grounds. *Interobang* was even printed on school grounds. Yet none of these papers were considered by the administration to be authorized publications of the school, and so none of them were censored. Unfortunately, very few administrations will make this kind of agreement with students.

I think it's true to say that most high school administrations try to suppress and sometimes destroy underground papers. In some cases, they have been successful. *Kaleidoscope,* of Appleton, Wisconsin, was stopped after the staff was threatened with suspension. Usually, however, students do not give up so easily, and my friends in Appleton tell me that they are planning to make a comeback.

The reaction from its readers has a great effect on an underground paper. A confrontation between the administration and the students can unify the students. Sometimes it impresses on them the idea that their paper is *needed*. *Mine*, of Tucson, Arizona, which is distributed in seven schools, confronted administrations several times. And the more some administrations tried to suppress *Mine*, the more the "miners" were determined to get their publication read. While *Mine* did not have too many problems in most of the schools, two students were suspended for selling it, and three times police have harassed "miners" for "blocking the sidewalk" and being a "traffic hazard." A student and the American Civil Liberties Union decided to sue Tucson District #1 for suspending the two "miners." Our different ideas of law and order.

Adults are often shocked by the underground papers, but the worst reaction usually comes in a fairly rural community—a community that is removed from the changing world and likes it that way. One day, suddenly, a group of high school students will awaken the community to their own world by producing not the harmless articles expected in an overground paper but the frank declarations of the underground. The paper is a concrete target, and the reaction may be violent because some people just don't like to be awakened. Ironically, this violent reaction usually only confirms the students' belief that the community—the adult community—simply doesn't know what's happening.

In Mahwah, New Jersey, a semirural community, several students caused a major controversy when they distributed 500 copies of their underground *Oracle*. Except for one four-letter word (shit), on page three, and a photograph of the back of an undressed Harvard student (which was taken from *Newsweek*), the *Oracle* was hardly a shocking paper—at least, I would have thought, to anyone with any claims to adult sophistication. Yet the community found plenty to be shocked about. The following is a transcription of what went on at the Mahwah Board of Education meeting on May 19, 1969, the day the *Oracle* was distributed:

CITIZEN X: I'm Mrs.[X——]. Has the Board seen this copy of this so-called underground newspaper?

BOARD TRUSTEE A: I had a chance, ma'am. (Indicates copy.)

CITIZEN X: Well, that happens to be my copy. My son picked it up off the ground today and brought it home to me and I've been sick ever since.

BOARD PRESIDENT: I was made aware of it at seven forty-five.

CITIZEN X: There is a nude picture of a male in the middle of this thing. There are words in here that are absolutely atrocious, and to me, it's one of the biggest pieces of filth I've ever seen. And I think these kids should have something done to them, before the younger ones get to see something like this center section. Maybe some of the parents haven't seen it, but there it is. (She displays it.) Picture of Harvard. Now I am just sick over the whole thing and I wish somebody would do something about this and including the page two, and I don't want to say the word but I will, it shows Mr.[M——], I believe, hitting a kid in bellbottom trousers over the head like he's God and the quote is "tired of the same old SHIT?" and it's signed by G. Dirt. Now is this something for young students to see?

BOARD TRUSTEE A: You very well . . .

CITIZEN X: Now may I ask what the school is going to do about this and not next Monday, I mean NOW!

TRUSTEE B: Well, all right, I haven't even had a

chance to read it. Seven thirty we were shown this. We don't have a crystal ball; we're just coming to the thing now.

CITIZEN X: You had it this afternoon. (someone coughs)

BRUCE AKIN (associate editor of the *Oracle*, has had his hand up since Citizen X first started to speak): Excuse me.

TRUSTEE C: Well it's delivered at the school to the children and we are no more than doing what we should be.

CITIZEN X: I agree. Bringing it up . . .

TRUSTEE C: Now we get in here at seven o'clock at night and convene here at eight, and we haven't had the time to look at it. Now I don't think the Board should be expected to come down with a guillotine. I think the Board should determine what its course of action might be to stop this, if indeed the Board feels it should be stopped.

CITIZEN X: Well, according to this, volume one, number one, and they state that they are going to put out more and they ask, "patronize our advertisers," and if you go into the back section there is a so-called advertisement with two telephone numbers and I have the telephone right here and I can give you the names of the people involved in this situation and they are students! They are not advertisers as far as I'm concerned. They are students of the school. They talk about pot. They talk about hadish [*sic*]. They talk about "G. Grass [&] Company, we carry the best line of pot this side of sunny Acapulco, mind-bending hadish [*sic*]—and colorful acids now on sale. Ask about our complete line of smoking accessories." This is right here in the paper.

BRUCE AKIN: Excuse me, Mr. President? Mr. President?

BOARD PRESIDENT: Just a moment, you'll get your turn. Ma'am, we understand your concern. Just let me point out one thing. Several members of the Board haven't even seen it yet. While there are those of us who have seen it, I have just seen the front page and so forth.

CITIZEN X: That even is a disgrace! Nobody wraps the flag around themselves!

BOARD PRESIDENT: I understand. It's just that it's difficult for us as a Board, when some of us have not had an opportunity to see it and discuss it, to make a comment at this time. We will discuss it; we will meet on it; and we will get the results. I think you'll find that it's impossible for us to say anything as several of us haven't even seen it.

CITIZEN Y (local John Bircher): Mr. [A———], your special meeting next Monday, will it cover this issue?

BOARD PRESIDENT: I would assume so, yes, because by then I'm sure we would have made up our minds. Yes.

CITIZEN Z: I just sat here and listened to our Superintendent say that he found two violations on this of Board policy. I cannot in my mind understand why a Board has to meet on it again if its policy has been violated.

TRUSTEE D: We don't. But we have a school administration.

CITIZEN Z: I can't see why there has to be any hesitation. If the Superintendent of Schools feels that there's been a violation on this piece of literature I don't see why the Board has to. They've already made their policy on it.

BOARD PRESIDENT: That very well may be, but we have not. Let me point out, we, the Superintendent of Schools has spoken to me as the President of the Board, referring the incident to me. It is impossible because of the nature of business that the various Board members are engaged in to get the Board together except to meet tonight. Several of the Board members are not aware of this problem. Now, we work as a Board and we've got a . . . (Tape ran out.)

TRUSTEE D: I said we are under instruction from the state Board of Education on the handling of protests, demonstrations, and that sort of thing. There is a good deal of research to be done before we flail out in all directions and, at this point, Citizen Z, nobody, I don't think, in this room, knows who precisely violated these policies. You might know, as we do, some of the people. They don't know them all, and we don't know the circumstances, and it's only, it seems to me, reasonable that we get a chance to go over this thing tonight and that the school administration get a chance to handle it without making it too big an issue.

CITIZEN Z: I'm not questioning whether it is or it is not an issue. My own feelings were . . . I had mixed feelings when I first read it. I'm only going on the statement that was made that it violated two Board policies. As far as I'm concerned, those policies were made. It's just like the police department saying "you ran a stop sign and a red light."

TRUSTEE D: Yeah, but he gives you a summons.

CITIZEN Z: Those policies are violated then, then those whose names show on the sheet as being editors-in-chief. At least you know they're guilty.

TRUSTEE D: But don't you get a summons from the cop and then go to court?

CITIZEN Z: Very true, but . . .

TRUSTEE D: Just give us a chance to write the summons.

CITIZEN Z: It doesn't have to go through the Township Committee before, right?

BOARD PRESIDENT: Based on the fact that in the eyes of the administration this was violating Board policy, the copies of the paper this afternoon were requested to be removed until action was taken.

CITIZEN Z: By all means. That's great. I just don't want to see something start snowballing here that the whole town's going to be sorry for, that's all.

HOW FAR SHOULD WE GO? 35

BOARD PRESIDENT: I understand your concern. Yes, sir?

BRUCE AKIN: My name is Bruce Akin and I'm listed in the *Oracle* as being one of the associate editors and I'd like to know if it would be possible. I talked to Mr.[G———] before about meeting with him later. I'd like to know if it would be possible for most of us are here who are on the staff of the *Oracle* to meet with the Board tonight to give them *our* views. We have good reasons why this was printed, and I think you should hear us out before you try to stamp us out, or kick us out, or do anything else.

BOARD PRESIDENT: I think until the Board has had an opportunity to review the publication and discuss it with the administration, it is going to be difficult for us to meet with you tonight. Perhaps a decision to meet with you later. But I think tonight the Board has a responsibility, the *whole* Board, discussing this situation with the Superintendent and reviewing the case before it can discuss it with you.

TRUSTEE C: I could be overruled, and I wish I were, because I hate opening a can of worms, and I smell that this is going to be a rather decaying can of worms. But I think the public's here, and they're interested in listening to this, and I would like to hear what sort of temerity these kids have that would call this something that is a responsible movement and something that they could do.

CITIZEN X: Right!

TRUSTEE C: And I think everybody else would like to hear it too.

TRUSTEE D: Well, may I say, that these kids are under age, they don't have counsel, they don't have parents with them in the main, and it is not fair to have these people make public statements which may be very damaging to them and their person.

36   OUR TIME IS NOW

TRUSTEE C: All right, I buy that.

CITIZEN Z: I think you're right, Mr. [Trustee C].

BOARD PRESIDENT: I would agree. I would retain that one prerogative. Yes, sir?

GENTLEMAN: While you're considering the newspaper, will you also consider this publication and see whether it violates any . . . (mumbles)

TRUSTEE D: That is before us too, Mr. [Gentleman]. That publication.

BOARD PRESIDENT: Yes, sir?

GENTLEMAN: I'm fine, thank you.

BOARD PRESIDENT: Are there any other questions from the audience? Yes, sir?

BRUCE AKIN: I think it might be beneficial if I were to read to the people here tonight the introductory remarks that we have in here.

TRUSTEE D: Mr. President, it's contrary to policy to demonstrate that thing, and if he wants to read it outside, let him read it there, but not.

BOARD PRESIDENT: No, I'm sorry, I'm not going to let him do that. (Citizen A and friend applaud.) Are there any other questions? Yes, sir.

JOHN CLINTON (editor of *The Virgin*): I just have one comment to make sir. My name is John Clinton. On the mobile hanging from the lamp fixture there we have a little card that says, if I'm not mistaken, "Be all you can be . . . READ." There is a caricature of the Statue of Liberty, and I don't believe that . . .

BOARD PRESIDENT: Sir, are you a student at Mahwah High School?

JOHN CLINTON: No, I am not.

BOARD PRESIDENT: Are you a resident of Mahwah?

JOHN CLINTON: No, I am not, sir.

BOARD PRESIDENT: Well, I'm sorry then, I'm not interested in your statement.

JOHN CLINTON: Very well, I . . .

HOW FAR SHOULD WE GO?   37

BOARD PRESIDENT: Yes, sir? Are there any other comments from the audience? May I have a motion to adjourn, please?

TRUSTEE C: I make a motion we adjourn.

The editors of *Oracle* were finally sentenced to "indefinite social probation," a sort of wishy-washy punishment. They soon came out with a second issue that did not cause nearly the scandal that the first one did. (There were no photographs.)

When you hear such opinions, you understand what the underground is up against, but the fact that the *Oracle* has been published in such a community today is the really significant point. It is a beginning. Things are happening even in a community like that, that wouldn't have happened fifteen years ago in a big city like New York. One of the main "gaps" between adults and the high school activists seems to be in their attitude toward ideas. We may not all be in favor of free love, but surely we should all be in favor of free thinking, but many adults seem to favor a repression of ideas that don't agree with their way of thinking. Not that they would ever admit it, but it comes out in their attacks on the young and their different attitude. It all seems to be related to the adult's frequent conflict between what he claims is his code of behavior—his beliefs—and his actual behavior. That's what causes a lot of confusion in the minds of the young.

Nothing infuriates certain adults more than a hint of blasphemy, and in an underground that often criticizes adults for being publicly religious and privately hypocritical, you're apt to get quite a bit of it, if only for shock effect.

American Revelation of Elgin, Illinois, ran a bogus "wanted poster" for Jesus of Nazareth:

WANTED Jesus of Nazareth

ALIAS—Subject is known to appear under the names "Son of Man" and "Prince of Peace."

VAGRANT—Loiters around synagogues; has a "hippie" appearance, often seen without shoes. Associates with common working people and the unemployed. Said to work sporadically as a carpenter.

ANARCHIST—Subject is a professional agitator wanted for sedition and conspiring to overthrow the established government.

CHARLATAN—Claims visionary ideas, said to victimize the sick and the blind with stories of miraculous cures.

MARKED—Scars on hands and feet the result of near execution by an angry crowd led by respectable citizens and legal authorities.

DANGEROUS—This man is a serious threat to estabished law and order. A substantial reward is being offered for information leading to his apprehension. If you see this man call your local law enforcement agency.

While this poster was obviously not directed against Jesus, the staff of the *American Revelation* told me that they received more objections to this poster than to any article they had ever printed.

Many adults have just as strong objections to obscenities, and some of them think all obscenities must be blasphemous. Some students see this as hypocrisy—that adults are disturbed by four-letter words in print while they use the same words orally. However, since obscenities are easily avoidable in most cases, the majority of the underground papers keep them to a minimum. Some of them even deliberately leave out all obscenities. They do this not because they see something wrong or immoral about four-letter words, but because such words alienate many readers—readers who otherwise might benefit from the content of the writing. *Links*, the "voice of the Wisconsin high school underground," is an example of a paper with no obscenities. As they put it, "we want to stimulate discussions on content, *not* language." A girl from Lake Mills High School expressed her attitude toward profane language in *Links*, as follows:

STICKS AND STONES MAY BREAK MY BONES, BUT WORDS ONLY CLARIFY OUR EXPERIENCE

LINKS
*Madison,
Wisconsin*

"Swearing is bad. It's an evil and useless way to express yourself. What's the world coming to when 10 and 11 year olds swear like truckers?"

That's what most of us have been told ever since we were old enough to consider doing it and even before then. To our parents, elders (?), and bosses (the Establishment), swear words are bad words. It's okay for them to swear because for them it's an established habit—hard to break. Besides, they're old enough.

Alright, let's pretend these are half-decent excuses and you ask one of these Great White Leaders why four-letter words are so bad. They will probably tell you something sensible and brilliant like this: "They are just wrong. And they're unnecessary, and (to whom it may concern) unladylike!" O.K., sometimes they are unnecessary, like when they are used just for the sake of using them, to try to show what hot stuff you're made of.

But what the hell's so right and necessary and ladylike about the four-letter words "kill," "rape," and "hate" and what they mean?! According to the dictionary to swear is to be profane. Since when are murder and rape good things?

Maybe if the words already included on the list of swear words are going to stay there, some additions

OUR TIME IS NOW

should be made, such as the ones above and many others.

It looks like they are right in one of their thoughts, anyway; what is the world coming to? And it looks like we have the answer: It's coming to us!!

Some students expect obscenities in a high school underground paper. Some seem to think that underground means profane. *American Revelation,* an Illinois paper that never has four-letter words, ran an article entitled "Why We Don't Use the Word Shit." The editors had been asked this question by so many students that they thought that an explanation of their attitude toward these words was called for.

WHY WE DON'T USE THE WORD SHIT

Many of our friends ask, "what's all this shit about no 'shit'?" Well it's like this, fans, if we used a lot of naughty words the Establishment would get all tinkled-off at us. Also there is a tendency for writers to use naughty words for the sake of naughty words which leads to poor writing, and we don't want any of that poop. However we realize some people see the use of profanity as the Ultimate Freedom. So as a public service we have provided a Do-It-Yourself Underground Newspaper Kit. Cut out each word below and paste it over a word in any newspaper or magazine, even *Revela-*

AMERICAN REVELATION
*Vol. I, No. 7
Elgin, Illinois*

tion, and presto! You have a dirty underground newspaper! So don't give none of your B.M. about clean language.

SHIT SHIT SHIT SHIT SHIT SHIT SHIT SHIT SHIT SHIT SHIT

Besides if this paper were meant for shit we'd perforate it.

Personally, I never really cared much one way or another about the use of obscenities in print until I put out *Smuff.* It was then that I realized the great effect a printed obscenity has. It seemed ridiculous, but one major interest of many students and teachers was to see how many four-letter words we dared to print. For this reason, we completely avoided offensive language in the first issue. In the second issue, the interview I did with the students in the high school commune in New York contained several four-letter words. I didn't edit them out because they were used effectively, as were the other words I left in the interview. Although the second issue was, in my opinion, better than the first, we received considerable criticism just because of these few words.

If an underground paper can't be suppressed, then adults often try to put it down another way. If it is well done and even they have to admit it, then they say it can't possibly be the work of "the kids." They accuse groups such as SDS of organizing small groups of high school students. You can see how wrong this is—how ignorant it is of the gap between the SDS generation and ours—by the interview with Robby Newton in the previous chapter. The truth is—as I've said—that in most cases where the SDS has tried to organize high school students, it has failed miserably.

In New York, when some people attributed high school revolts to the influence of "adult revolutionaries," an underground paper, *The Observed*, made this response.

IN ANSWER
Claire and Nina

THE OBSERVED
Vol. I, No. 4
New York

According to Superintendent of Schools, Bernard Donovan, and President of the Board of Education, John Doar, recent disorders in the city schools have been instigated by "revolutionary adults." They claim that outside agitators have directed and financed the violence in the schools. They also claim to have evidence proving this, but refuse to disclose its nature.

To Mr. Donovan and Mr. Doar, we have evidence proving that we, the students, have proudly planned, directed and financed these uprisings, based on our *own* "revolutionary tendencies." We ourselves have organized a student union to represent and defend our views. We ourselves have painstakingly raised the money to support our cause. We ourselves have published and distributed leaflets and newspapers. We ourselves have fought for the rights denied us. Do not give the credit to outsiders!

Appearing on "Searchlight" on WNBC-TV, Doar urged such methods of dealing with violence as meeting with the school officials, getting the truth, and communicating it to the students so that rumors do not grow.

Yes, Mr. Doar and Mr. Donovan, let us act to improve school conditions. But intensified regulations and putting more cops in the schools will not do it. In your own words—let us get to the truth and communicate. (Together we shall win?)

Student uprisings are, of course, the result of the students' own "revolutionary tendencies," and although their goals are similar, the leaders in the high school underground often have little more than these "tendencies" and their culture (youth) in common. Adults often talk of student "rebels" as if there's some one type, as rigid and unchanging as a car off the assembly line, responsible for every underground act. As a matter of fact, I haven't found a stereotype personality anywhere among the student leaders I've met. I think of adults trying to make, for example, Ross McConnell, a student from a high in Columbus, Ohio, into one of these stereotype "rebels." Impossible. Ross, who is editor-in-chief of *The Guilded Bare*, also plays football at his school, and this has caused a conflict of interest. When I met Ross, he said that he knew his football coach would give him a choice between football and the underground in the fall. Ross had wanted to continue both activities. (His last decision, as I understood it, was to play football in the fall and then to go on radicalizing the school after the football season.)

This is likely to be a common problem, because a student who has enough interest in his school to work on an underground paper is likely to be involved in many other school activities as well. But contact with students with similar problems in other parts of the country is definitely an encouragement in deciding to resist the opposition and its subtle attempts to make you give up. More and more editors are exchanging papers, corresponding about techniques of protest and reform, and meeting when they can. When it appeared weekly last spring, the *High School Independent Press Service* sent news, cartoons, posters, editorials, and photographs to about 100 high school underground papers.

Sansculottes, one of the first and most impressive of all the underground papers, was started to serve the community of the Bronx High School of Science, but as it grew—an average issue included sixteen pages of newsprint—it branched out to other schools. Yet, after thirty-one issues, the staff closed down *Sans*, because they found a more effective way to serve the school communities and "dissolve into the twentieth century." Their explanation also illustrates students' readiness to change even in the face of success, which is one of the characteristics that give their movement its strength.

A LITTLE BIT OF OVEREXPOSURE

SANSCU-LOTTES
No. 28
New York

In light of the recent exploration by the editors of this newspaper into the psyches of teachers, I felt that for the conquest of ignorance and the betterment of mankind, a similar work should be initiated concerning the personalities (and other abnormal manifestations) of these same editors. As Freud analyzed Freud, *Sansculottes* analyzes *Sansculottes*.

No newspaper is complete without a fiery editor-in-chief, and Paul Steiner fits his role well. In the tradition of Perry White, he torments his staff to such an extent that it is surprising that a readable newspaper is ever produced. Exuding calm, self-assurance in public life, his private existence is racked with hypertension and insecurity.

His relations with the other members of the staff are about as dogmatic as his inner struggle to maintain his outward cool. As general distributor, David Graham is subject to harassing phone calls in the dead of night, and public condescension (much to the chagrin of his loved ones). Michele Goldfarb, given the impossible task of reaching someone who didn't have a phone, was ready to assassinate—yes, assassinate—the cause of her troubles: our coordinator. Other examples of Herculean feats assigned to the over-worked staff are: the construction of a library to house all the back issues of *Sans*; the sculpting of a 120-ft. statue of Paul, to be erected at the Pentagon after his death; and paying him monthly tribute so he won't write articles like this one about us.

Enough for Paul Steiner. The rest of the staff is imbued with its own problems, ranging from messianic desire to see one's name in print to paranoid reticence to attend the weekly meetings.

I am forced at this time to make my readers aware that nothing in this report can be held against the editors (in any way, shape, or form) as specified by Blackmail Code #60317. Thank you for your understanding.

My associates assure me that nothing is worse than psychoanalyzing struggling artistry. Upon their suggestion I will stop. But first I must tell you that if there is anything, anywhere, anybody in need of psychoanalysis, no force in heaven or on earth will impede my flight to their side.

SANSCULOTTES DISSOLVES INTO THE
TWENTIETH CENTURY

This is an age of simultaneous, spontaneous action and communication. An age of electronic immediacy. Of constant crisis. It is extremely hard to relate a monthly newspaper to this kind of situation. And an established, "solid" paper like *Sans* is necessarily distant from its readers. It is impossible to have a participatory newspaper. Decisions must be made, skills must be taught, articles must be edited, and on and on. There is most definitely a clique, even if it's open, of the *Sans* staff. There has to be a close-knit group to put out a readable paper. And that group is bound to be resented by those who aren't in it, simply because it exists. There is no need for that kind of resentment or the hierarchy that causes it in the high school radical community. *Sansculottes* has served the movement for over three years. If the movement has grown, *Sans* has helped its growth and grown with it. If the movement has changed, so has *Sans*. *Sansculottes* has educated, organized, radicalized, turned on, awakened, and become a part of many lives. It can continue to do so. Or it can try to do more.

The radical community at the Bronx High School of Science is a large one. It has a responsibility to the other students. It has accepted and generally carried out its responsibility, but it should do more. It must do more if it is to put an end to the niggerization of the minds of students. A radical self and social realization of what's going on is the first and most important step towards changing it. We must try to bring

MAMA
No. 1
New York

this about at Science (where most of our staff are doing time).

Now we get to what you've all been waiting for. Issue number 31 is the last edition of *Sansculottes*. We are merging with our community. We will still be dealing essentially with the printed word; it is, if you will, "our thing." What's going to be happening is a constant communication of our thoughts, feelings, dreams, ideals, ideologies, and realizations. It will be on all levels. Purpose: to present and build upon alternatives to the current system of basic exploitation and alienation. Big words are ambiguous—specifically we will print analysis and artwork, poetry and news, rock criticism, draft-birth control-health-living advice, theater-movie-book-reviews, and more. It will be directed at Bronx Science students and will try to directly involve them in its production. It will be distributed (free) in school every day or two as a two page thing. It will be an extremely immediate educational experience. The structure of its production staff will be defined by the structure it assumes. It's very hard, if not impossible, to describe exactly what it will be like because it will be a communal voice of very separate and variously developed individuals.

Yes, we are copping out on the other schools. But if we are going to have any real effect, if we are going to build a radical high school movement, we will have to focus on our own student communities at our own schools. We will have to educate and involve students as directly as possible. We feel that this is the best way.

Why are the activists the minority? One answer can be found by looking at adults—very

OUR TIME IS NOW

few of them are activists, and they have more to react against than we have because it is their world and they are supposed to have the power. Another answer that I have heard is that most high school students are just as conservative as ever. This I doubt. Of course, many students are conservative, but they are not the majority. Their number is diminishing as the radicals increase. The majority are simply apathetic students who don't care very much what happens as long as they stay out of trouble. If these students are conservative, they don't care enough about their school to be actively conservative.

In the following article, which appeared in *Links*, a student radical talks about and to the majority.

THE APATHETIC MAJORITY

LINKS
*Madison,
Wisconsin*

The apathetic majority are usually those people who fear active participation in any movement outside and sometimes even inside the system. Their reasons for this are very often real and legitimate. The following article will attempt to explain what, in my opinion, causes such widespread apathy and indifference toward working for any kind of change.

The first and, unfortunately, biggest reason is parents. Most high school students (in my school, anyway) come from middle and upper class homes and conservative parents who don't want to lose what they've "worked hard all their lives for" just because of a "few misguided radicals."

Young children are easily influenced by their parents.

After living 15, 16, or 17 years with parents who rarely get involved in anything and condemn those who do, it is easy to see why apathy occurs.

There are always some kids who get radical in spite of, or possibly because of, their parents. But even they are sometimes hesitant toward any action because of what their parents would do if they found out.

Another major reason for apathy toward major change is that, although they don't like the schools any more than we do, they don't understand exactly what we're doing. A lot of this is our fault because of our inability to communicate with other students about what we're going.

Social life is another very definite cause of indifference. So many people consider their date on Friday night more important than the war in Vietnam, poverty, racism, hate, and the lack of freedom in this country for the reason that their date has a *direct* effect on their lives whereas these issues don't (wait until the draft board gets you).

This isn't to condemn social life or to say we shouldn't have one. Obviously we should, but it can get to the point where social life is the prime concern and that's a bad scene.

Then there are the people who are too hung up on themselves to give a damn about anything else. This reflects the tragic paranoid influence our society has on its people. Kill or be killed! Nobody else is gonna care about you; you gotta care about yourself!

A few kids are apathetic because they fear freedom, but these are in the minority. In the school system we have now, all or most of the decisions are made for us. This is fine for the person who can't make decisions and doesn't want to take responsibility for his own life. It provides security.

A large percentage of the indifferent don't care because they don't think it will do any good. They don't expect the administration or anybody else to even listen to them, much less take them seriously. The main reason for lack of recognition is our small numbers (which, after all, really aren't that small) because of student apathy. Even one or two more students becoming active make a lot of difference. So join us! Don't be the subject of this article, because if you don't dig what's going on in our schools, you can do something about it.

A Student of Monona Grove H.S.

IS THIS THE BEGINNING OF A NEW UNDERGROUND ?

DIDN'T YOUR MOMMY TELL YOU NOT TO TALK TO SEWERS ?

JUST WHO IS THE MYSTERIOUS BEAU TYCOON ?

Now I've HEARD all this NONSENSE about the STUDENT as a NIGGER! About 'em having no rights and no protection and so-called student-teacher SEGREGATION and I just want to get a few blasted things STRAIGHT! I mean I guess I KNOW my STUDENTS!

Firstly, let me say some of my BEST friends are STUDENTS and BASICALLY you couldn't WISH to meet a more POLITE, RESPECTFUL, HAPPY lot when they know their place. Why some of 'em are even quite ATTRACTIVE... (chuckle) Yeah!

With their own kind they seem to ENJOY themselves IMMENSELY... dancing (got a lotta rhythm!)... wearing gaudy clothes! We TEACHERS say if you could be a STUDENT just ONE Saturday night you'd NEVER want to be a teacher AGAIN! (chuckle) And they're VERY good at SPORTS!

cartoon from US

But GOSH DARN it some folks talk about 'em like they were US! And FACE it, what contribution are they making to the ARTS? How many DOCTORS, LAWYERS and BUSINESS LEADERS are STUDENTS? Biologically they're just not EQUIPPED to handle FREEDOM and POWER! How I envy them!

So these OUTSIDERS who try to STIR 'EM UP over RIGHTS and such are just making TROUBLE for EVERYBODY! First thing they'll want to write on every line and use staff washrooms and call us by our FIRST NAMES! And brother, there's NOTHING worse than an UPPITY STUDENT!

And just between us would you want one to marry your daughter?

Ann Arbor, Mich.

An important function of the underground press is to make people aware of how bad the condition of the students is today. Through the press, students must make adults aware of their lack of freedom and how it restricts their learning. If they don't, the adults may never think to give students their

THREE The Student as a Nigger

freedom. And, perhaps even more important, the underground must make the majority of *students* aware of their condition. While many students don't like school now, too many of them think that this is because learning simply isn't meant to be fun and there is nothing that they can do about it. As a result, they are apathetic. By making these students aware that learning not only can be fun but it *should* be fun, the underground papers must change this.

Today, much of the learning that goes on in the high schools is a result of discipline. The students are learning facts because the teacher is telling them the facts, and if the students don't learn the facts, they will fail the test. And the students respect the teacher and the tests because they are taught that they will be punished with a bad future career if they don't.

Nothing is wrong with discipline, and nothing is wrong with facts. However, an educational system should not be based on them, as it seems to me ours is. It seems as though every time a school starts an activity that could possibly encourage thinking, they blow it.

Student councils could give students a chance to experience the power that people in a democratic society have and thus cause the thinking and discussion that naturally come after such power has been granted. But the schools blew it by only going half the way and constantly holding veto power over the councils. And obviously school newspapers could provoke thought in both the students who read them and the students who put them out. But the most profound thinking that high schools encourage in this area is thinking about why the principal is censoring the newspaper. In many classrooms, discipline is used to excess, so that learning history in high school is like learning how to salute an officer in the army. And while they are using this discipline to excess, teachers and administrators often naturally start to treat the student as a lower form of human being. This can be seen in the halls when an administrator is yelling at a student who would like to explain but knows that the administrator will just become more angry because a student is daring to talk back to him.

Is the condition of students really this bad today? Of course it varies. "The Student as a Nigger," an essay by Jerry Farber, which originally appeared in the *Los Angeles Free Press*, gives one answer that expresses the sentiments of the high school underground. Farber says, in effect, that being a student and hating school is as justifiable as being black and hating slavery. He points out how few rights students have in school—that they are, in fact, second-rate citizens. He shows how the student is expected to "know his place" when dealing with a professor, how professors use weapons such as the grading system and absurd dress restrictions to keep the student "in his place," and, worst of all, how the students take it.

Farber makes a big point about teacher-student relations. He shows how concerned teachers are with holding the students' respect and thus retaining their identity as teachers. To me, this seems to have a great effect on students. It restricts them to their present role as high school students when this isn't natural for them as human beings. We are all both teachers and students. Of course, separate teacher and student roles must be created in a formal education situation. But a good teacher should be flexible and willing to switch roles with the student.

Although Jerry Farber is a professor at Berkeley, and his essay actually concerns college students, "The Student as a Nigger" can be more easily applied to high school students. Most college students are in school by choice. High school students, however, are forced by law to remain in school until they are sixteen. And while college students may not have enough freedom and power, high school students have far less.

Obviously, the analogy between students and niggers is meant to emphasize how bad the condition of students is by exaggerating it. The treatment of Afro-Americans in this country has always been far worse than the treatment of students. Slavery was never meant to benefit the black man, but to exploit him. Admittedly, high schools do benefit students in some ways; they do learn something. But this analogy was meant to provoke thought about the condition of the student, not a discussion of the racial situation in the United States.

Since it does so effectively provoke thought about the condition of the student, "The Student as a Nigger" has become a recurring theme in the high school underground press. Farber's essay has appeared in more underground papers than any other single article. The idea of the student as a nigger has been brought out in other articles in high school underground papers.

These articles are written primarily to make the students aware of their slavery and to remind them that the time to fight for their rights—their life—is now.

The reason why "The Student as a Nigger" is an effective essay is that it can be applied to so many situations in school. I have often heard both teachers and students make reference to it. (The essay had been shown around by several students, and it was later printed in *Smuff*.) Once *Smuff* publisher Bob Cohen and I went to the faculty lounge to talk with a teacher. The teacher motioned with his hand for us to come in when he saw us standing in the corridor by the door. As we entered the room, he noticed strong signs of disapproval on the faces of the other teachers in the room. So, instead, he came out and talked with us in the hall, laughing and saying, "You niggers had better stay here where you belong; the next thing we know, you'll want cushioned seats like we have in the faculty lounge."

Other articles in underground papers that express the idea of the student as a nigger are also effective. In *Smuff*, we ran two short articles entitled, "Why Students Are Being Thrown Out of School." They weren't editorials and only stated facts as simply as possible. The articles were effective for two reasons. First, they showed how the administration was abusing its power of discipline. And second, they pointed out to students that they could expose such abuses any time they felt that their rights as students were violated. By using the underground press, the students could take this step toward liberation.

In many ways, Farber is right. Students are niggers. The underground papers have supplied the evidence, as in the following examples. The first article shows that students have tried to work with the little power that has been given them and have discovered that even this is phony. The other articles almost form a serial, the continuing story of "The Student as a Nigger."

THE GAME IS OVER

T.R.I.P.
Vol. I, No. 5
Long Beach,
California

Once upon a time a couple of naïve, innocent editors of a high school underground paper and a few of their friends decided to try a small but very educational exercise in democracy at their own school. They wanted to use a democratic process called the "power of initiative" to put proposals on marijuana and Vietnam on the school ballot so that the kids at their high school could vote on issues which were important to them and to the world around them, just like grown-up people do in real life. They wanted to do it right, of course, so they looked up the law on initiatives in the Student Body By-Laws (which seemed so much like the Constitution that grown-ups use) and found out that signatures of 10 per cent of the Student Body on a petition were enough to put any measure on the ballot. So, the editors and their friends set out to collect the required signatures in order to place their initiatives on the school ballot. A lot of people told them that they were crazy, but they were determined to show everyone what wonderful things could be done in a democracy, so they refused to give up.

The editors publicized the initiatives in their underground newspaper, and after a while they counted the number of signatures they had collected and discovered that they had over 100 more signatures than they needed. They were very happy with their overwhelming success and rushed to the Student Council of their school to show them the petition and tell them the good news.

But the Student Council already knew all about the petitions (some members had even signed them), and they had already discussed the matter when the happy editors came to them with the petitions. The Student Council told the editors that they had decided by a vote of thirteen to four that the initiatives could not be put on the school ballot.

"That's not fair!" said the bewildered editors. "It doesn't say anything in the Student Body By-Laws about the Student Council having to agree to put the initiatives on the ballot. It says in Section IV that signatures of 10 per cent of the Student Body are enough by themselves to put them on. You don't have any right to keep our initiatives off the ballot—that's cheating!"

The Student Council listened to the poor editors' pleas, but they refused to change their minds. The editors, who were very upset, decided to take their problem to the principal of the school. They had positive proof that the Student Council had cheated, and they were sure that the principal would help them.

The principal was a kindly, white-haired man with a big smile. The editors told him all about what had happened, and showed him exactly how the Student Council had cheated. They asked him to tell the Council to play fair, and to let the marijuana and Vietnam initiatives on the ballot. The principal listened carefully to the editors' story, and they had a long talk about it.

Many things were discussed, and the principal said many things, but what he essentially said was, "Now, now, boys, I'm sure you have had a lot of fun, but I think this whole thing has gone a little too far. You must remember that although you have your own Student Body By-Laws and you get to elect a new

Student Council every semester, which is very educational, I am the principal, and I have to do what is best for the school. You should know that when the Student Body By-Laws say you can put any measure on the ballot, they don't really mean it. We can't have important issues like Vietnam and marijuana on the school ballot. Besides, the Student Body might vote in favor of legalizing marijuana—just think what that would do to our image! It's lots of fun to play democracy, but the game has gotten a little out of hand. Now, I'm sure you can find other things to do at this school, and when you grow up you can start all the petitions you want."

At first the editors were terribly shocked and disturbed by what the kindly principal had told them. But then they realized how foolish they had been to pretend that their high school really was a democracy. They realized that they should have known that the principal would never let their initiatives on the ballot, because they had broken the unwritten rule of the game: "Thou shalt not rock the boat." The editors swore to themselves that never again would they let themselves be fooled into thinking that a high school is a democracy instead of a dictatorship.

There is a moral to this story. If you are a high school student, and you think that your high school is a democracy, you had better take another look. You don't really think you have any Constitutional "rights," do you? Of course not. If you want to have freedom of speech, freedom of the press, or any other freedom, while you're in high school, you'll have to use methods other than "proper channels." Either you can do something unethical, like starting an "off-campus" underground newspaper or jumping on a soap box when nobody's looking and yelling "Lyndon is a fink!" or you can just sit around and wait until you graduate and they release you into the outside world.

MYSTERIOUS CHANGES IN STUDENT BODY BY-LAWS!!

T.R.I.P.
Vol. II, No. 2
Long Beach,
California

Two amendments have appeared mysteriously in this year's edition of the Ram-Pages. In the 1967 edition, two sections of Article IV of the By-Laws read:

Section I: Any member of the student body shall have the privilege of initiative. A petition signed by 10 per cent of the student body shall be sufficient to bring to vote *any* new measures.

Section III: In case any step taken by the council is unsatisfactory to the student body, a petition signed by *10 per cent of the student body* shall be sufficient to bring the measure to a vote of the student body.

The sections this year read as follows:

Section I: Any member of the student body *who has cleared the topic with the principal,* shall have the power of initiative. A petition signed by 10 per cent of the student body shall be sufficient to bring a vote on this new measure.

Section III: In case any step taken by the council is unsatisfactory to the student body, a petition signed by *20 per cent of the student body* shall be sufficient to bring a vote on this new measure to the student body.

This new version claims that initiative petitions must now have principal approval *in advance* and that the referendum petitions must now have twice as many signatures.

By definition, both these changes are *amendments.* According to Article VII, amendments must be ratified by the Student Council. A careful check of council minutes has revealed neither change has ever been ratified. Mr. [X———] told T.R.I.P. that the change

OUR TIME IS NOW

in *Section I* was made by him and was not an amendment. This is hard to understand because a change in an official document is defined as an amendment.

Mr. [X———] knew nothing about the amendment to *Section III*. The printer has reported that the spelled "ten" could not become "twenty" by any mistake of his.

Whoever made the second change has not yet admitted to doing it. Rumor has it that the proofs for the Ram-Pages made just one stop between the activity office and the printer. It has been speculated that Mr. [Z———] made that second change. The latest announcement was by the Student Council, stating that the change in Section III is void because it was not ratified.

CENSORSHIP IN SCHOOL PUBLICATIONS

Two years ago, A.H.S. finally regained a newspaper, which was badly needed. Good, but its function has been, we believe, so constricted by censorship that it does little to reflect opinions of the students it so eagerly sought to serve. Almost every teacher in any administrative capacity has his say as to what will appear in the pages of *Crimson Chronicle*. The result is often a watered-down version of what the writers produced.

COMMON SENSE
Vol. II, No. 1
Alton, Illinois

The reason for censorship as it has come down to us is that a newspaper can be dangerous, especially in the hands who might have a tendency to disregard "policy." Our school system fears criticism or any statement that tends to contradict administrative "policy" or step on any ideological toes. They are trying to make the system appear monolithic in thought when it is not and never can be. They believe that anything controversial or able to be interpreted as controversial has no place in a student publication. Thus the paper has become in its editorial outlook little more than an outlet for this "policy." This is not realistic in context with our society; it is a crime. Perhaps the censors have a point, but not to the extent they now practice. The question is whether the article could be interpreted as slanderous or incorrect, but not whether it is controversial or dissenting. Controversy is the raw meat a student must feed on to become intellectually mature.

Generally good judgment is used by the staff as to what is printed. Students on the whole tend to be wary of producing insults to authority in their writing and seldom abuse their right to speak freely. Nevertheless by the ever present blue-pencil coercion of the censor, the urge to think about controversy and express dissenting thoughts in print is stifled. Of course administration should have final authority to say when a statement is improper, but in our opinion they have perhaps drawn the line too thickly and have been too wary of any dispute the paper might cause.

It is easily seen what this censorship has done to the paper's context. If a copy is analyzed, it becomes apparent that most of it is trivia, or holds to "policy"; and one would never know there are people thinking, really thinking, at that school. This lack of content is a direct result of fear of censorship by school authorities.

Two articles written by a high ranking *Crimson Chronicle* staff member failed to reach the presses because their contents were considered too controversial. To define "controversial" in this sense means these articles did not follow the administration's monolithic policy and therefore found their way to the waste paper basket. This is only one example of the administrators' common practice of censorship.

The right to dissent (and it is a right) has been

severely limited in student publications. In the end, it comes to this: Through censorship of ideas in our school, are we producing automatons to conform to the "line"? (Or should we produce people who are capable of creative, individual thought?)

These are the facts as we see them. If the facts have been misused, or the administration would like to clarify its position, please feel free to use this paper.

EXPLANATION PLEASE

COMMON SENSE
Vol. II, No. 1
Alton, Illinois

As most people know, A.H.S. student schedules are arranged by IBM computers. This is the excuse usually given for the rejection of a schedule change after the first of school. Other excuses are: "You're picking teachers," or "There is no room" or "The principal says no!" and many more are given by counselors, teachers, and administrators. This is not fair! A student should be entitled to change his schedule when necessary. The student's education should not be limited by his class arrangement. If a class is not conducive to study or learning for him, it should be changed, and the student should not be given excuses why the change cannot be made. There cannot be that much trouble and bother to change a schedule. For example: If a student doesn't like a teacher, any educator is aware that he won't make much of an effort—so why not change him? There may be some difficulty concerned with the change, but the results will justify the trouble.

As the situation stands now, the school is run for the convenience of the IBM computer, not the student. The answer to this problem is simple (why it hasn't been done already is puzzling). There must be an explanation of the scheduling system and excuses by the administrators to the teachers and counselors, so that students can understand this "unnecessarily complex system." If everyone has an understanding there won't be resentment and confusion with the current system of scheduling.

OUR PATRIARCH
J. P. and B. Barrett

FREETHINKER
Vol. I, No. 2
La Puente,
California

Would William A. Workman be allowed to attend Workman High School?

According to the rules set down by the establishment, our opinion is NO!

As most of you know, suspension notices are given to students who do not abide by these rules. On page 28 of the Workman Student Handbook, under S.D.R., it states that a haircut should begin at the bottom of the ears and be tapered up. But on page 14 of this same publication, there is a picture of William A. Workman, whose appearance is not in accordance with this rule. Yet the school is named after this "undesirable." Mr. Workman's hair seems to be hanging over his ears.

We feel to alleviate this problem the school should be entitled "Yul Brynner High" or a new dress code should be adopted.

The choice is yours.

OUR TIME IS NOW

ILLEGAL SEARCH AND SEIZURE

With full knowledge of some of our administrators, girls' unlocked P.E. lockers were searched the week before last by the P.E. faculty. Those who had cigarettes in their possession were either suspended or warned. The compensation to the students was that the cigarettes were not taken away (as if this were an act of generosity).

FREETHINKER
Vol. II, No. 1
La Puente,
California

The lesson to be learned, said the administration, was for the students to lock their lockers. This is incredible! If someone (a student) were to steal from one of these girls' purses, the administration would punish them severely. But the administrators are the people who are going through their purses, saying the lockers were unlocked in the first place. It's as if someone could rob your house just because it's unlocked. They are clearly in violation of the Fourth Amendment which defends "the right of the people to be secure in their persons, houses, papers, and effects. . . ." They should either take their history lessons over again or be punished for their actions.

FREE SPEECH AND ASSEMBLY

Since when did students get punished for things they talked and thought about? One has to commit the crime before he is punished; he cannot just *intend* to do something.

FREETHINKER
Vol. II, No. 1
La Puente,
California

On Wednesday, the 13th, a student was suspended for asking another student if he was going to participate in a walkout. They *hadn't* walked out and the suspended student did not even ask him to walk out. By the First Amendment of our Constitution, no one has the right of "abridging the freedom of speech, or of the press; or the right of the people peaceably to assemble. . . ." If our administration can get away with this, the next step might be taking away eye contact between students. This has already been tried. The aforementioned student and her sister were told by an administrator not to look at each other while making a decision about their walking out.

THE ODYSSEY OF MARTY COHEN
Marty Cohen

THE OBSERVED
Vol. I, No. 4
Flushing,
New York

If you would like to know just how screwed-up our school's gym department is, listen to this.

On Thursday, March sixth, I came into second period gym as usual. I dressed, and went in to play volleyball. At the end of the period I went back into the locker room. I found that my sweat shirt, laundry bag and a can of deodorant were taken from my locker (borrowed is the word the gym dep't uses). The normal procedure is in this case, to report to the teacher in charge. I walked into the gym and Mr. [Z———] informed me that Mr. [X———] had a monitor taking out any clothing that he found in the small lockers and putting it into the lost-and-found.

With this knowledge, I went on to my next class, confident of getting my stuff the next day.

The next day, I went to school with a cold, and was excused from gym. I went into the locker room, and found Mr. [X———]. I asked him if I could look in the lost-and-found for my stuff. Politely, he opened the lost-and-found and said his monitor had taken the stuff I described to him. Looking around, I found my stuff. Just as I was about to leave he said, "O.K., that will be 50 cents!" Astonished, I asked him, "What for?" He replied that he couldn't give it to me unless I paid him. "This is ridiculous," I told him. He replied that it was "Tough luck." He didn't make the rules! I told him I wouldn't pay, and proceeded to walk out of the locker room with my "borrowed" articles. Becoming annoyed, Mr. [X———] asked me who I thought I was, and I replied, "A student." Once again he said he couldn't give it to me until I brought in the 50 cents. I replied that I would not pay him, because it was his monitor who took my stuff in the first place. Mr. [X———] then said that it was for my own protection. I replied, "In the future, please don't protect me so much!" He then exploded and said, "Are you telling *me* what to do?!" I told him with a hint of anger in my voice that I was not telling him what to do, and that I began the sentence with please.

Mr. [X———] then said, "You little joik, what do you think I'm trying to do, steal your money?" I said, "More or less, you are." He then got even madder and said, "Now you're accusing me of stealing your money." I told him that first of all, I was directing my statement to him as the spokesman of the gym dep't, and second of all, I never used the word steal! He said, "Stealing your money, huh!" and proceeded to show me a book full of receipts from other suckers who paid to get their rightful possessions. He asked me if I would rather have someone else steal my stuff. I said yes, because it would be done by some degenerate and not by a school *official* who was supposed to set an example. He then hit me over the head with his stapler and said, "You little joik, you see Mr. [Y———]!"

I got a pass from Mr. [O———] and went to see Mr. [Y———], semi-confident that he would see my point.

I walked out of the gym with my pass and saw Mr. [Y———]. He greeted me with a smile which soon faded. He asked me what was the matter and I warmly told him. He said I'll have to see the teacher in charge of the locker room who just happened to be Mr. [X———]. I said that Mr. [X———] had told me to go see him. He asked me what happened and I related to him the events preceding our meeting. It was at this time his warm smile turned to an angry frown. He said that I would have to pay (I said to myself "Not this again") and I replied I would not pay to get back my possessions which were taken from me by a monitor for the gym department.

His words which followed I don't remember exactly but what he said more or less sums up to—tough luck kid, go see Mr. [X———]!

I returned to the gym and went up to see Mr. [X———], who said he couldn't do anything more for me. Mr. [Z———] asked me what happened and I told him. He said, "If I were in your place I know what I would do, but I am in no position to be able to tell you. You'll have to use your own judgment." I thanked him and went back to sit in the rear of the gym.

At the time of this writing I still have not gathered back my stuff and I will probably end up paying the money.

What I would like to say now is that if there is any high school official (hopefully Mr. [A———]) who sympathizes with my points, would he *please do* something to rectify this situation in the future for students who will fall into this swindle.

NOTE: We urge all students to look into where this 50 cents is spent. We don't know—do you?

ANOTHER CASE OF AMERICAN JUSTICE

HIPS
New York

      This story took place in June of 1968 and it may be rather out-dated. But remember! It can happen any time, any place, on any terms.

 Robert A. [Z———] was a student at the Brandywine High School in Brandywine, Delaware, before he was thrown out of school and arrested.

Coming from a rather unpleasant home life, Bob had managed to get through almost four years at Brandywine before he committed his two major sins. First, he let his hair grow long. This constitutes a crime anywhere in this bourgeois American society, but in status conscious Brandywine it is a felony with overtones of homosexuality, heresy, and high treason. Bob's second offense was to begin selling the *Heterodexical Voice* (Delaware's underground paper) around Brandywine High. Everyone knows how those "Commie-rat bastards" are trying to destroy the wonderful educational process down in Newark and caution is great in Delaware high schools, lest the minds of our youth become subverted and they start attacking the secondary educational system (which of course does not need attacking because it is already perfect). Robert [Z———] must have failed to see the logic, or must have joined the ever growing number of America's youth who see the sterile life it portends. The "push-comes-to-shove" law went into effect.

About two weeks before school was to end, the principal of B.H.S. called Bob to his office and put down the law. "Bob, you've been in a lot of trouble. We don't want you at commencement exercises." [Z———] then mentioned the most obsolete word in America today. He tried to invoke his "rights." The honcho's reply was predictable. "You don't know what your rights are. We don't want you back." Bob was informed that his diploma would be sent to him later. Later in the day, [Z———] discovered that all "longhairs" at Brandywine were receiving the same treatment. If commencement at Brandywine were not to be just, it would at least be attractive to the spectators. Bob returned to the office to question the good principal on the matter. Having failed to get a confession to sin number one, the principal brought up sin number two. The administrator knew that he was selling the now infamous issue number four of the *Heterodexical Voice* and "if you come back tomorrow, we'll have you locked up." The next day Bob returned.

During the second class period, Bob left his as-signed study hall and went up to the library. The vice-principal saw him and ordered him to go down to the office. At that time, according to Mark Kenneally of Brandywine High School, students were prohibited from leaving either study hall (which had been moved to the auditorium) or the library. Kenneally was in the hall already, however, and saw the ensuing confronta-tion. Bob was met at the office by four of Delaware's finest. They were there to arrest him for trespassing. Kenneally was able to see one of the four cops choking Bob as he held onto a chair and said, "I'm not going." The fuzz had different ideas and, after he passed out and was handcuffed, they took him to Court 15 where he was charged with assault and battery against a police officer, trespassing, resisting arrest, and (the librarian managed to throw this one in) distributing obscene literature. The trial was to take place in the court of Common Pleas; the Honorable Robert H. Wahl was presiding.

The rest of the story goes on along similar lines. Bob needed a court appointed attorney, who just happened to disagree with Bob's views. At their meeting, he told Bob, "I don't like your kind."

At the trial, the assault and battery charges were dropped and Bob pleaded guilty to trespassing and resisting arrest. That left only the obscenity charge. Judge Wahl said what he thought of the word "m.f." (nice people never say "motherfucker" except in certain designated areas, like locker rooms). Bob responded with a statement that most of us could agree with. He said that there is "no such thing as obscenity, only obscene minds." He also stated that he believed in the Bible and, if we accept what was written there, we might all be considered motherfuckers (an interesting thought, Cain and Abel had no sisters). Bob's logic convinced Judge Wahl. It convinced him to find Bob guilty and send him to two psychiatrists. The sentence came to sixty-five days.

So remember, this story is potentially that of anyone in America who tries to do his thing. Play ball or get fucked. That's America, kid. That's where it's at.

ARMBANDS

Do you know how the administration tried to justify its action of ruling out armbands? In the words of Assistant Principal, Dr. Kean, "These armbands have polarized the Workman High School

FREETHINKER
Vol. III, No. 1
La Puente,
California

campus, leading to disagreements and fighting." But is this any reason to ban armbands? What if it did polarize (divide) thinking on Workman campus? This is just what the armbands demonstrated. Well, what then? Would Dr. Kean outlaw thinking—as he tries to do when he tells us not to say anything against the administration or demonstrate thinking to the contrary of the administration? All this just goes to show that this administration does not want any real thinking on this campus—they don't want students to take opposite sides on anything that really affects their own lives. School is not made for us to really think: It is made so we swallow the "learning" that is spoon-fed to us, as we proved when for just once we started thinking for ourselves.

WHY STUDENTS ARE BEING THROWN OUT OF SCHOOL

SMUFF
Vol. I, No. 2
Hackensack,
New Jersey
On Thursday, June 5, Gary Kole, a senior at Hackensack High School, was sent home from school because an administrator did not like his pants. At least, that was the technical reason.

The administrator began by telling Gary that his pants (which, incidentally, were not dungarees) were faded in the back. The administrator went on to say that he did not like his general appearance.

Just as he was about to let Gary go, the administrator noticed a Magic Marker drawing of a ship on the back of Gary's hand. When he was asked what it was, Gary responded, "That's the Titanic."

Gary was then sent home to change his pants.

On Friday, June 6, Christopher Galfas, a junior at Hackensack High School was sent home for cutting a class. At least, that was the technical reason.

According to Christopher, he was going outside to cut a study when he was approached by a member of the administration. The administrator asked Christopher where he was going, and Christopher replied that he was going outside because it was too hot to sit in study. He went on to say that the school should give more responsibility to students and that the school system was "antiquated." The administrator responded to this by saying "Go eat prunes" and sending Christopher to the main office. Although Christopher was going to cut class with several other students, he was the only one who was sent to the main office. Christopher was then sent home. Mrs. Galfas was telephoned and told that her son was guilty of "cutting class and sarcasm."

AND STUDENTS SUSPENDED

Three Washington Irving girls have been suspended, for refusing to surrender "multiple copies" of the *Weakly Reader*. On May 14, they were told to leave the papers with Mr. [X———], when they entered the building after distributing them outside. They refused, claiming that the administration had no legal right to confiscate private property, which is true. Mr. [X———] refused to allow the girls to attend classes. He then got a call from the Board of Education, telling him that he couldn't prevent them from attending classes unless they were suspended. So he then suspended them. The Board of Ed by-laws state that no

WEAKLY READER
No. 14
New York

student is allowed to leave the building without parent notification. Mr. [X———] overlooked this, even though he met with the parents of one of the girls an hour later on PTA business. The girls have been allowed back to school, after signing an agreement to surrender "multiple copies of publications" in the dean's office when they enter the building. The girls and their parents are now suing Mr. [X———], charging him with refusing to allow the girls to carry their personal property, for violating rights guaranteed by the United States Constitution, and for sending them out of the building without notifying their parents.

BEHIND BARS

UP AGAINST THE WALL
Vol. I, No. 11
Southhampton,
New York

Ever notice how much Southhampton high school (or any other high school) is like a prison? Why you can't even go to the lavatory without first begging for permission and assuring the teacher that it is "necessary." Just as in a prison, you are forced to take abuse from anyone "in authority" without complaint, knowing that to do so would only invite punishment. You are expected to be docile and obedient cattle who unquestioningly act, look, and think according to the school's wishes. In short, the school allows you all the personal freedoms that any well-run prison would.

Of course, you know that all of this could be changed. By sheer weight of numbers, the student body is a powerful force to be reckoned with. If it were organized, there would be no limit to what could be accomplished. Take dress codes for example. How long do you think that the ridiculous law against slacks and culottes for girls or blue, the color blue, jeans for boys would be in effect if two or three hundred students came to school wearing the "forbidden" clothes? Or, what about those boring assemblies which are forced on us without our consent? If those same three hundred were to boycott or walk out of a boring, irrelevant assembly, the administration just might get the message. If the school is to be run for our benefit, we should start exercising our power as students.

Did you ever wonder why the barbed wire on the fence around our school is facing inward?

JUGENDBE-WEGUNG
Downey, California

Of course many students do not think that their school is like a prison. These students have "school spirit." But if you asked someone in the underground movement, they would be likely to say that these students have been "brainwashed."

WE'RE NUMBER ONE (BOOM), WE'RE NUMBER ONE!
Miss "Iace Hoc Ad Illi"

On the 16th of September, I entered Millikan High for the first time, along with some thirteen hundred other sophomores. We were all nervous, all bright-eyed and freshly scrubbed, and all of us were

T.R.I.P.
*Vol. II, No. 2
Long Beach,
California*

scooping in first impressions as fast as possible, because we each wanted to be the first on his block to act nonchalant and experienced.

But my first impressions were probably different from the average, because I was stuffed to the gills with cynical, worldly disdain. I was fully prepared to sneer at pep talks, cheerleaders, and the school paper. However, because I am thoroughly open minded and willing to be proven wrong, I was equally prepared to find that "pep talks" are worthwhile speeches, cheerleaders fun, and the *Corydon* a vehicle for serious news and views.

I was pleasantly surprised at the opening day assembly by Student Body President Mike Lipson's speech, and even Mr. Wood's speech, contrary to my expectations, was quite devoid of the usual what-a-great-student-body-you-are and what-a-great-year-you-are-going-to-have soap. But my peace of mind was shattered Friday, at the sophomore assembly. The climax of the impressive ceremony came when everyone chanted along with the cheerleaders, "We're number one! We're number one!" punctuated by the boom of the bass drum. For a moment I could have sworn it was 1984, and the middle of the Two Minutes Hate. That's the kind of school spirit cultivated at Millikan—blind, automatic, and meaningless.

As for the school paper, it was the identical, inane throw-away our junior high paper was, and it tries its best to drum up school spirit, too.

I wouldn't want to fall into the category of those who criticize without offering constructive alternatives. But the only really constructive alternative to brainwashing is no brainwashing. So, first of all, let's not have any more of those revolting pep talks, and lay off the yells. They're all right for football games, but not for the auditorium. And let's not have any more of this school spirit business. Isn't Millikan good enough to inspire spirit without stupid chants?

Let's use the time for something else. Propaganda we can do without.

Unfortunately, students who blindly accept school policy are too often the ones who get into student government organizations. This is one reason why many students have contempt for their student council. They see it as an "Uncle Tom" organization serving the administration—not the students.

But even if the student governments were run by students who wanted to invoke change, they would still be inadequate. As Jerry Farber says, they are "toy governments." In many schools, the student council is really just a pacifier for the students; it makes them think that they are doing something to change the school. But the contempt that some students show for the student council proves that it is no longer an effective pacifier.

INTERVIEW
Rich Shadden (R.S.)

Once again *Minstrel* sends out one of its roving reporters to interview people that affect your everyday life. Today our reporter is interviewing Sy Cofant, the president of the Student Council. (Ed. note—Yes, Virginia, there is a student council.)

MINSTREL
Vol. I, No. 4
Waukegan,
Illinois

REPORTER: Sy, you were elected president of the Student Council last year. Was it a close election?

SY COFANT: No, it was a landslide in my favor. My two opponents and I campaigned for the same thing but my name was first on the ballot and therefore was the natural choice when no one could tell us apart, which was most of the time.

R: We understand there was just a 15 per cent turnout at the polls. How do you account for this?

SC: Good luck, I guess. We expected much less because the cafeteria was serving chocolate chip cookies. That's the reason I didn't vote, but the cookies were well worth it.

R: Many of the students you represent are beginning to believe that the Student Council is a powerless figurehead set up by the administration. What are your views on this subject.

SC: It's a lie. None of the 15 per cent I represent believe this. And the idea that Student Council is powerless is ridiculous. Look at the power I have, I preside over all the Student Council's democratic meetings and recognize any speaker I want to. I get to ask everyone to stand and say the pledge of allegiance at assemblies and sometimes I even make a speech before the whole student body.

R: Remarkable!

SC: And if anything goes wrong, I get to tell everyone over the intercom system, if Mr. NO lets me.

R: You truly have power. Doesn't all this power frighten you?

SC: Sometimes, but I try to live with it. I watch myself and try not to misuse my power so Mr. NO won't take it away and give it to the student paper.

R: What important decision have you and Student Council made this year?

SC: Well, let's see . . . ah, we decided to have dances for the students.

R: Is that all? I mean students have dances every year.

SC: They do? Oh yeah, we decided to have a concert with Hector Heathcoat and the Merry Marimba Band.

R: But I thought they couldn't make it.

SC: You're right, but you asked about decisions we had made, not things we had done.

R: Many students don't believe this school should have a dress code. Do you believe there should be a dress code?

SC: Positively! I don't know what I would do if the administration didn't show me how to dress, I'm *only* 17. After all, the administration did kindly consent to teach us and I think we are obligated to be taught their way. Anyway, why all the trouble. In a year or two they can dress the way they want to in the army.

R: Your logic astounds me.

SC: Thank you.

R: Thank you for your time and for the interview. Good afternoon.

SC: Oh, that's OK. This was just Student Council homeroom and we don't do anything anyway. Goodbye. Did I sound right, Miss Less? Mr. Poverty, I've got to go to the potty.

OH PLEASE, JIM!

In another few weeks an era will have passed. The Ding-a-Ling dynasty of Jim Anderson will be over. How can we ever forget his guiding leadership that helped us live our lives as best we could in these troubled times? Who can forget his booming confident voice informing us over the intercom that another Student Council event has been changed? In our hearts we will always remember the strong, patriotic way he led us in the pledge of allegiance. It's almost time to say goodbye to a leader so widely acclaimed and near-

MINSTREL
Vol. II, No. 1
Waukegan,
Illinois

unanimously elected (17 per cent?). Oh Jim, tell us, what can we do without you? Think not only of us, but of Miss [O——], too. Who will be around next year to add those little pleasures to an old woman's life? Jim, don't go! But if you must, *take that goddam Student Council with you!*

Which cleverly brings us to the point of Student Council. No matter whether you believe in student power or not, Student Council is an insult to your intelligence. The administration tells us that it is a representative body, elected by us to govern student affairs. How many people voted in last year's election? Less than 20 per cent. One fifth of the students of W.T.H.S. chose the officers of S.C. You might say it's the other's fault for not voting. But popular opinion seems to believe that S.C. is a lost cause and not worth taking the time to vote. This is a well placed belief.

If we examine four events that concerned Student Council in the past year, we can see how truly inefficient it is. First of all there is the decision not to give the Student Organizing Committee a club charter. The vote was 24 to 0. SOC had at the time a membership of close to fifty members, all students of W.T.H.S. That would mean the club would have been one of the largest active clubs in the school. However, Student Council felt the goals of SOC, i.e. to promote democratic processes, were a duplication of their own goals. Therefore, SOC was not chartered. Perhaps another reason S.C. didn't bestow a club charter on SOC is because Student Council is a major target of criticism by SOC. The second event in our study of Student Council is the instituting of open discussion meetings. In October the first meeting was held. The purpose of the meeting was to allow S.C. and the administration to find out what the students were thinking. It seems this project worked too well; the second meeting in November was the last. It seems Student Council and the administration (they go hand-in-hand) didn't like the way students were talking about their gripes and making others aware of the situation as it really exists. The situation started getting involved. I guess S.C. decided that was bad. Out of one of the open discussion meetings came the Dress Code Committee. Its purpose was to examine dress codes at other schools and make a recommendation to Student Council about our own. Its recommendation was the elimination of our dress code. The Student Council (in one of their great displays of wisdom) went for an administration-backed "itemized" dress code. Finally, there is Turnabout. It was a social activity planned by Student Council. This is the purpose Sue Walden in a recent issue of "W" World gave Student Council: planning and sponsoring social events. Well, that's all fine and nice and everything, but how many people go to dances like Turnabout? Twenty-five per cent? That's a thousand students; it's less than that. So Student Council exists to plan social events for a minority of the students. That's a far cry from the representative governing body the administration says it is.

Student Council couldn't do anything against the administration even if it wanted to. Mr. [X———] has a total veto over S.C. and he's not the only one. Mr. [Y———] has too. Even Miss [O———] has a psychological veto. If she doesn't like something, the trend is for S.C. not to like it, either.

If you don't feel Student Council should be replaced, you should at least feel it should be done away with. It's a fraud perpetrated on a minority of students. So please, Jim, take that goddam Student Council with you. pleasepleasepleasepleasepleasepleasepleaseplease

GIRLS' DRESS

FREETHINKER
Vol. II, No. 2
La Puente,
California

At the end of last year, the Girls' Dress Board met and invited students to join its next year's activities. Staff members of the "Freethinker" went to observe how this "democratic" dress board was conducted.

When we arrived, very little was said (a lot was mumbled) except that the advisor was "surprised" to see us. We then asked the requirements for joining, and were informed that the individual must be accepted by their "group" (of popular soshes) and must dress neatly! We questioned how the students were represented if all members of the board were picked by this small group. The advisor said she "hoped" these students would take suggestions from the girls of our student body to present at their meetings. Not much was said (except that these girls could report any student not dressing "properly" to the Girls' Asst. Principal without having the accuser's name mentioned or having to face the "accused"). Then a "Freethinker" suggested pants and shorts for everyday use. She felt this would solve the "step problem" as well as "role playing." However, this was rejected by a member of the board because "What would we have for Bermuda Day?" The advisor said it would not work because the students "were of a low intellectual level," besides, in 1945 (I forget exactly the date) it didn't work at such-and-such college (!). Students, this is a "representation" of "your" opinions!

RULE OF THE 'MAJORITY'

COMMON SENSE
Vol. II, No. 1
Alton, Illinois

The true power of Alton Senior High's Student Council was recently demonstrated. The Council, in effect, voted three times to eliminate the cheerleaders from being candidates for Homecoming Queen. A special meeting was held to inform the Council that their proposal did not meet the administration's approval. The administration further stated that the Council's measure would *not* be allowed to stand. Once again 'democratic' principles are put to practice at Alton Senior High School.

WOOD CHANGES POSITION; STUDENT COUNCIL GIVEN RUN-AROUND

T.R.I.P.
Vol. II, No. 5
Long Beach,
California

Reversing a previous stand, Mr. Wood has said that, in spite of the overwhelming vote by Millikan students in favor of a one-month moratorium on dress regulations, he will not support the move. Mr. Wood stated that the PTA Board and a group of parents, the Lay Advisory Council (the members of which he refused to name), had stated that they were opposed to the one-month moratorium. Mrs. Sprague, president of the PTA, denied that the PTA Board had opposed the one-month moratorium.

Neal Phillips, Long Beach Director of High Schools,

said he feared he might lose his job if the one-month experiment went wrong. It is now regarded by the members of the Student Council who have been most interested in dress regulations as probable that the one-month moratorium cannot be achieved this year, and quite possibly never.

Sometimes radical students object to favoritism that they say the administration shows toward "good niggers" as opposed to the students who are getting "uppity."

FOOTBALL FUN

T.R.I.P.
Vol. I, No. 6
Long Beach,
California

A shocking scandal has been revealed at Millikan.

A certain group of students at Millikan is being coddled by the administration. This "group" is the school's football team.

The incident in question occurred earlier this year. A number of football players in joyous "celebration" wrecked a bus, causing $600 worth of damage. Normally, one assumes, the people responsible would have been severely reprimanded, perhaps suspended, for this senseless vandalism. Instead, however, the school only required that the football team "pay" for the damage. This in itself is damning. The really outright favoritism,

OUR TIME IS NOW

however, occurred in the so-called method of payment. Instead of the offenders splitting the cost individually, the funds from a "Sports Night," held on school property with the aid of school advertising, went to pay for it. If a group of science students, however unintentionally, damage a piece of school equipment in an experiment, they pay for it out of their own pockets.

This type of cover-up is inexcusable. The money from Sports Night could have gone for some far more useful purpose (like jockstraps for the tennis team).

As if all this weren't enough, there is strong evidence that the football team is only paying for part of the damage. In conversation with a student, Mr. [X———] stressed the importance of the football team's trying to pay, which strongly implies that they did not pay all of it. In addition, there is the *fact* that the Sports Night netted *less than one-half of the $600 needed to pay the damage!*

Finally, there is a rumor going to the effect that the student body is paying the rest of the tab. If true, it would constitute a supreme indictment of the administration. The school authorities should be called upon to answer this charge with a yes or no reply.

Millikan cannot tolerate a special license for certain students to be vandals. This type of incident could, in the immortal words of the Student Council, ruin Millikan's IMAGE!

Of course, there are the nigger-loving teachers—the teachers who believe that the schools should be run for the students. James Horelick, an English teacher at Washington Irving High School in New York, seemed to be a nigger-lover. But Mr. Horelick no longer teaches here. He was fired. The following article explains why.

During his brief teaching career in New York, Mr. Horelick made his apartment available as an office for an underground paper, *Weakly Reader*. He also helped to put the paper out and even gave the paper monetary support when it was needed.

At the beginning of the next year, after a legal battle, Horelick was rehired.

ANOTHER NON-STRIKER GETS THE AXE!

WEAKLY
READER
No. 13
New York

Mr. James Horelick, English teacher at Irving for the past three years, has been fired, and will lose his teaching license in June if the Board of Education supports decisions already made. Mr. Horelick explained to the *Weakly Reader:* "I am a regular teacher of English, on probation. This means that after this year I would have been sure of a job at Washington Irving until the year 2013. I was relieved from having to consider such a possibility when I received a special delivery letter—twelve hours before the time limit expired —which informed me that my service this year was unsatisfactory and that I was not recommended as a teacher here next year. Among other things I was accused of having sold a copy of the *Weakly Reader* in school.

"This is certainly a singular distinction, and whenever I think about it I become so overcome with emotion that I'm speechless, which is just as well, because the matter is being heard at the Board of Education on May 14; I will say that the school PTA has written asking that the decision to fire me be withdrawn, and that I be allowed to remain at Washington Irving.

"No it wasn't a complete surprise. I've had the feeling ever since the strike ended that you're damned if you do, and you're damned if you don't. I did and I was. If I do lose my case and have to leave Washington Irving, I'll miss the girls, many of whom have become real friends in these years. But you do get a little sick of constantly being regarded as 'The Enemy.'"

CASSELL REFIRED

One hour after being suspended, Mr. Landman, as a parting gesture, wrote a letter re-assigning Miss Ruth Cassell of the Washington Irving English department to JHS 22. She also received a letter from the Central Board of Education re-assigning her to Washington Irving. She received a third letter, special delivery at 3 a.m. Saturday morning, also written by Mr. Landman. The third letter re-assigned her to JHS 60, and was written after Mr. Landman had been suspended. On Monday, February 3, Miss Cassell reported to Irving for the first day of the new term. When she showed her letter from the Central Board of Education, Mr. Oak said, "It's a mistake, get out of the school." She left, and has been teaching at JHS 60. She says that she is so disgusted with the entire situation that she will probably quit teaching. Mr. Oak's gain has been the students' loss.

WEAKLY READER No. 10 *New York*

HORELICK VICTORY

NEW YORK
HERALD
TRIBUNE
No. 7
New York

James Horelick, the Washington Irving H.S. teacher who was recommended to be fired for having sold a copy of the *Weakly Reader* in school last year, has won his fight to keep his job. At a meeting of the members of the Board of Education on August 20, it was unanimously voted to reject the findings of Dr. Donovan, and voted instead that Mr. Horelick be transferred, with tenure, to another school. It had been suggested that he be transferred with a reprimand, but after he and his attorney presented their case, the reprimand was abandoned. Mr. Horelick has not yet decided to what school he will go, and is considering suing the Board to block his transfer.

Mr. Horelick explained his position: "The common assumption is that the transfer is to appease the principal's union, an organization devoted to the preservation of the power of a bunch of ten-cent hacks. The union may run the Bd. of Ed., but it doesn't run the courts. Since I received no reprimand, the implication is that I did nothing wrong. If this is so, then there was no reason for the transfer. Let's not forget that the 3-month strike of last year was about the issue of involuntary transfer of teachers, presented under a smokescreen of firing and due process. I guess it's one thing when it comes from the Board and another when it comes from the community.

"It's been suggested that the transfer is due to a personality conflict between the principal and me. Nonsense. Mr. Oak was careful to state in his testimony that he was not harassing me because I was a non-striking teacher, but would act against any teacher who sold the *Weakly Reader* in school. I have no criticism of him. Last year was a bad year. Let's forget the bitterness. I hope that when I return to Washington Irving, we'll all work together for a happy school."

And in conclusion:

STUDENTS AS CATTLE
Mike Fox

THE OBSERVED
Vol. I, No. 4
Flushing,
New York

This summer I worked on a farm; being an "Aggie" and coming back to Bowne I noticed a number of corollaries between the cows and the students here.

The first is that the farmer doesn't give a damn about his cows. He cares only when it involves the cows' milk production. The only time Farmer [X———] cares about us is when it involves our production. We produce marks and grades instead of milk. We are also bred for further production outside of Bowne. When a farmer notices that a cow isn't producing well enough he "calls" her out and sells her to the slaughter house. In the same way we are called out after Bowne, into college, and remain with the herd or into the army to be slaughtered.

The greatest similarity is feeding time. The cows are herded into the barn, crowded together outside a little door where they have to go in slowly, one at time, just as we are crowded in front of the lunchroom door, where one of Farmer [X————]'s helpers check our program cards. Once in the barn the cows are locked in—we are locked also. We are cows. The cows are then led out in a herd and back into the field. They can't leave the herd because the doors are locked to keep us in. The cow has no recourse to abuse by the farmer. We have no recourse to abuse by the teachers. The cows have numbers and records which are carefully kept. We have delaney cards and transcripts, also carefully kept. The cows live a carefully regulated day, never asked what they want to do, but told, just as we are told.

Cows are very stupid animals. They accept their fate and will always continue to do so. A cow is huge and the farmer small. There are 30 to 60 cows, but only one farmer, but alas, cows are poor dumb animals and can't get together. We can. We don't have to get milked anymore if we don't want to. The time has come to get off the farm. The time has come to unite and struggle together. Burn the barn and get out NOW!

"High school students are gettin' together" is a statement that is found in many high school underground papers and in almost every issue of the *New York High School Free Press*. The slogan is not original; a version of it has been used in the black-power movement. However, it does express an important part

---

FOUR   Mobilization: Gettin' the Students Together

---

of the high school movement. If high school students do not get themselves together, they have no movement.

The press is the most effective tool that the high school underground has to mobilize students. The papers themselves serve as advertisements for the movement. The ideas they express and the opinions they hold both tell the students something about the movement. When the papers tell the students that they are niggers or cattle, the underground is trying to make students aware of the need to get together. This is the first step. After that, the press can unite the students by showing them concrete programs that will change things. The program can consist of an attack on part of the present educational system that the students want to be abolished. Dress codes, censorship, and disciplinary measures are three examples. Or the program can be centered around an outside-of-school program that students can learn from and enjoy. The activity can be a film festival or even a student-run course. What it *is* isn't as important as what it is *like*. The activity must be exciting, educational, and worthwhile because it is fun. If the students don't really want to take part in the activity, it has no reason for being.

Since *Smuff* was started near the end of the year, we didn't have time to concentrate on instituting this kind of program to mobilize students. This year, however, some such programs are being initiated. This year's staff intends to hold a film festival at the local Y.M.H.A. They hope to rent some films from Newsreel, an organization that rents radical films. Also starting this year will be an entirely student-run independent study course. So I will have to look to the future to see how well these activities mobilize Hackensack students.

The mobilizing methods that revolve around programs are usually meant to muster support from the general student body. They are not expected to be very successful in recruiting students to *work* for the underground movement, helping put out a newspaper or organizing future activities. The best way to get students to actually work together is to actually get them started putting out the underground paper.

Naturally, we had to do this to get out *Smuff*. We got people to work on *Smuff* by simply making them aware of it. We put out a first issue. The first issue was not too ambitious, but it was enough to get some other students interested in working with us. We put the first issue out with little help and with few contributors. But by the time we were finishing our work on the second issue, we had help from several more students and we had many more contributors.

Then we came against a new problem—keeping the *Smuff* spirit alive over the summer. Teachers speculated that *Smuff* would die out after Bob Cohen and I graduated. And we expected that we would have a difficult time disproving them without putting out *Smuff* ourselves again the following year. We had successfully organized students in 1969. Would this organization survive through 1970? Well, it did. The first issue of the

1969–70 school year came out with new ideas and new programs for the new year. Bob and I did not have too tough a time, because Edd Luwish and several other students thought it was well worth reviving after the summer.

Maintaining support for the underground movement is a job that is tackled differently by different papers. A way of mustering support that is used in many underground papers is a form of advertising. For example, *Think*, a "Youth for Peace, Freedom, and Justice Newsletter," from Royal Oak, Michigan, ran an ad that said, "Girls: do you worry about the color of your hair? the style of your clothes? . . . Do you suffer from bad breath? Just remember: *struggle makes you gorgeous!*" This ad was as much for entertainment purposes as for advertising. It is a humorous approach that is taken by many underground papers. The ads do not result in the deeper support that comes from getting involved in the underground press or in a program for students, but they do catch the attention of the reader.

Weakly Reader also ran a general ad for revolution:

IT'S AS AMERICAN AS . . . "MOM"

Stuyvesant!! The perfect school! The epitome of AMERICAN know-how! Why, where else could you find:

—a knowledge-tight assembly line that moves the product from junior high school to college with a minimum of contamination by education

—2500 well-oiled walking talking eating wetting moving parts—guaranteed to jump at the boss's command

WEAKLY
READER
No. 13
New York

—a sellout union in full (almost) control of its faculty

—spot-checks, speed-ups, lock-outs, grade slavery, suspension of Constitutional rights fobbed off under the guise of "liberal education" and benevolent paternalism always so profitably employed by Big Capital.

And it's 99 44/100 per cent PURE (LILY-WHITE).

Well, Brother, that doesn't sound so great to us. We're sick of slavery, this contract to spend four years of our lives training to throw away the rest. We're obedient little niggers that Massa whips with grades, darkies who jump when the Man says Jump! We're sick of it —students, workers, blacks and oppressed people everywhere: We're going to claim our birthright—dig that Manifest Destiny—we're going to be Americans and what's more American than REVOLUTION?

We're getting together—pulling together for our human rights and needs—and it's time that you are either WITH us or AGAINST us!

We demand:
 —Open Admissions to Colleges
 —No Suspensions or Expulsions
 —Freedom of Speech, Freedom of the Press
 —Establishment of Black, Puerto Rican, and
  Radical Studies Courses
 —End to the Tracking System
 —Cops, Narcos, and Security Guards OUT of the
  Schools!

WE'RE MAKING A REVOLUTION—JOIN US!

Stuyvesant Radical Coalition

The *Weakly Reader* "ad" for revolution is general, but it ends with seven specific demands. By listing a seven- (or ten- or twelve-) point program, the high school underground unites the students with common goals. These demands from the *Weakly Reader* outline the program for the Stuyvesant Radical Coalition.

Stating demands can be an effective method of organizing students, but it also tends to hurt communication between the students and the administration. One mistake that is often made by students is to refuse to compromise on demands. Because of this, administrations call the demands and the students unreasonable. Another problem is that these demands are called demands and not requests. The word "demand" backs the administration into a corner.

The students who most often use the word "demand" are also the ones who use words like "struggle" when they refer to the underground movement. They see the administration as the enemy, an enemy that they don't mind backing into a corner.

Although making demands does hurt communication, the students who make demands can easily be defended. Often they have tried making requests and working through the student council, and they have discovered that "playing by the administration's rules" doesn't work.

The following letter explains a little further why students resort to making demands:

Dear LINKS,

A few students of D.C. Everest High School, Schofield, Wis., came to some rather controversial conclusions this fall—controversial simply because they happened to disagree with conclusions previously held by the Administration.

LINKS
Madison,
Wisconsin

We "happened to notice" the utter disregard of students' rights; partly manifested in our rigid dress code. We "happened to notice" the suppression of free and unconforming thinking. And—worst of all—we couldn't "help but notice" that this type of atmosphere was condoned by the Administration and employed by the majority of teachers.

Knowing that the Administration and faculty would never agree to our conclusions and resulting proposals, we decided to work among ourselves, the students. We decided that apathy about our situation had existed far too long, and that some action should be initiated immediately.

Here are a few examples of what has happened to us in our fight at D.C. Everest:

1) After months of "negotiations" with students, faculty, parents, and Administration, our new dress code completely disregarded most recommended changes which students had made;

2) Attempts to circulate materials resulted in threatened suspensions;

3) The creation of a civil rights bulletin board resulted in criticism ("Why are *you* interested in civil rights?");

4) The selling of underground newspapers and "Black Power" buttons resulted in a suspension;

5) Lockers were and are searched for "condemnable" materials;

6) The formation of a high school SDS group resulted in an Administration conference for every student in attendance at one of our meetings;

7) Students selling underground newspapers were sent to the school psychologist;

8) Students who wrote into newspapers criticizing the dress code were called into the office—if they had enough guts to sign their name;

9) A student was relieved of a Student Council pass,

although activities that were supposed to have taken place under that pass were never proven;

10) Those leading the movement were and are subject to hours in the Administration's office;

11) And the writing of this letter will provide impetus for a headhunt that would be terribly funny if it wasn't so pathetic.

This middle class suppression has been allowed to exist far too long. They have done enough to us, but not quite enough. Those who continue the fight will subject themselves to the label "communist" (which we have been called), and to pressure and investigation not unlike the McCarthyism of the 1950's.

Their hostility is incredible. Their tactics are as dirty as ours are labeled to be. The searching of lockers and personal possessions, the tracing of out-of-school activities, the request for names in return for clemency—it's an endless list, all supposedly in the name of "the educational system."

Is it too much to ask—to be able to criticize our educational system without apologizing? Is it too much to ask that those who hold accepted norms be questioned?

Yes, we at Everest guess it is. So we're not *asking* anymore, *we're demanding!*

> By the Brothers and Sisters
> of D.C. Everest High,
> Schofield—Wausau.

Leaflets are effective student mobilizers. Along with the underground papers, they present immediate issues that range from dress codes to capitalism. One of the most entertaining leaflets I have seen was distributed in Madison, Wisconsin, during a janitor strike. It follows.

Also following are articles in various underground papers, which bring up issues that are useful in mobilizing students.

GARBAGE

LEAFLET
La Follette High School, Madison, Wisconsin

This leaflet is about our school. This leaflet is about garbage. Let it collect in the hallways, classrooms, bathrooms, Mr. Wendt's office. Let it pile up till they have to close down the school.

Then the city will be forced to deal with the janitors who are on strike demanding a decent wage.

The school administration wants us to help pick up the garbage so that school will look clean and neat. But don't take garbage from anybody. Let it all hang out! Garbage is reality. Let's show what our school is really like.

Support your local janitors' union in their just strike. Do not work against their strike. Do not pick up the garbage!

When you finish reading this leaflet, tear on the dotted line, fold, mutilate, and drop it on the nearest floor.

Sometime, the strike will be settled and all this garbage will be cleared away.

OUR TIME IS NOW

BOYS' DRESS CODE

During the past year a group of students sent out a petition asking the Administration for a more lenient dress code. The petition was signed by the majority of the students. The administration rigged a meeting of "representatives" of the students. Half of our "representatives" did not show up for the meetings. It may not have been very important, anyway, because Mr. Faul had to approve anything the group decided. The "representatives" were chosen by the teachers and not by the students. This year we are not going to ask the Administration for a new dress code. Let's tell the Administration that we are going to have a new dress code WHETHER THEY LIKE IT OR NOT!!

FREETHINKER
Vol. II, No. 2
La Puente,
California

TACTICS FOR THE FALL
(*Editorial*)

The most basic problem facing us is how we can transform this society into one where all people actively participate and benefit from their work and the work of their fellow man. Capitalism will soon face a severe crisis. It desperately needs a continuation of the War in Vietnam or a War somewhere else. The cities are quickly boiling over and if a massive program of urban renewal is not started soon there will be a tre-

ENRAGÉ
Vol. I, No. 2
New York

mendous explosion. However, there is no money available; discontent among working people is rising rapidly. Purchasing power of the average production worker and non-supervisory worker has gone down, while inflation and taxes have been increasing at a phenomenal rate. The ABM program which will bring short-term gains to the corporations may well be disastrous in the long run. The inflation index is rising and the ABM will speed this up, thus precipitating a money crisis in an already shaky market. Inflation (which is due to profit-push on the part of corporations [1]) has brought about more strikes and a greatly increased trade-union militancy and with this, a new student-worker rapport.[2] In addition, capitalism's need for constant growth to increase profits necessitates a society based on consuming goods produced. Movements against this society's materialism and the infusing of new ideas which could lead to questioning the basis of this system are suppressed more and more, while increasing numbers of people become aware of the irrationality of this system.

The moment for action is coming soon and when it comes, students must be prepared. What is needed now is two important things:

1) Critical study of the nature of this society. We must "capitalize on what has taken place (French May–June revolution, Columbia tactics of '68 and '69, Harvard, etc.), analyze it theoretically and prepare to resume action." [3] We must attempt to define the type of education we want. "By criticizing what is, we shall finally define the themes of the ideal University (and High School). We know that the University (and H.S.)

[1] See June issue of *Monthly Review* for an article on inflation with a table that indicates the actual decrease in purchasing power that has occurred in the past four years.

[2] See the June issue of *Independent Socialist* for articles on the Bethlehem Steel and Chrysler strikes.

[3] *The French Student Revolt: The Leaders Speak.* Daniel Cohn-Bendit interviewed by Jean-Paul Sartre.

is not an entity bearing no relationship to the society in which we live; on the contrary, it is part of it. The University cannot be changed without changing the society to which it is adjusted. Better functioning forms of the University (and H.S.) are realizable; they would be better adjusted universities (and H.S.'s), not ideal ones." [4] This we must realize—that the type of education that we want simply cannot come in this society.

2) We must organize ourselves into a loose organization, somewhat analogous to the March 22 Movement in France. An organization is necessary because students must have some cohesiveness and must take concerted action, not loose guerrilla-type action. This organization should not be a vanguard, like the Bolsheviks, but one in which a significant number of students participate and one which is capable of being a catalyst. Leftists today make up a minority in the schools, though a significant one. We must unite NOW, and adopt an ideology and agitate and organize other students.

When the time comes we must be ready. All students must see that their interests do not lie in maintaining this society and must be ready to build a new and better one. ALL POWER TO THE IMAGINATION!!!

OPEN CAMPUS

In the primary grades we were often blessed with a thing called "open campus," but now that we have matured they have taken this away from us. We either have to eat a stale sandwich from home

FREETHINKER
Vol. II, No. 1
La Puente,
California

[4] *Ibid.* O. Castro (M22) on Round Table discussion on Radio Luxembourg.

or eat the school's "Skippy's" meat loaf. Why can't we eat a decent hot lunch at home? Aren't we supposed to have more rights than a third-grader? We are given harder work and more responsibility; we should be given more privileges, not less! We are now in a situation in which many students of Los Angeles City Schools are walking out to protest such treatment, and they are getting new administrators who sympathize with their grievances as a result of their militancy! Don't you think we should ORGANIZE to get a grievance system that can get results and a sympathetic response to our needs the present administration is incapable of?

They won't even let us ORGANIZE: They call it "agitation" and those who do it "trouble-makers." Their approach, by this technique, is "Divide and Conquer" by handling people individually and throwing all their weight and rank against them, instead of respecting our right to act in unison, which they forbid. Our motto therefore should be "Unite and Conquer."

Another campaign that got students together, working for a common goal, was the campaign against suspensions. Leaflets were distributed and the campaign was publicized in several underground papers. This campaign was part of a program for students to "protect each other" from people they consider to be their enemies—the administration of their school and the police. Students were letting each other know what to do when they get busted by their school or by the police.

END SUSPENSIONS NOW!!
Dana Driskell

By June, 1969, at least 40,000 and possibly as many as 50,000 students will have been suspended in New York's high schools. This figure represents a 300 per cent increase over the number of suspensions last year. It also indicates the number of students who are not willing to accept the man's bullshit any longer. The more students willing to go out on a line for their rights, the quicker they are ready to endure expulsions, suspensions, and the administration's other tools of repression, the sooner this racist educational system will crumble down around the pig's flat feet.

Last year the vast majority (90–95 per cent) of suspended students were black. They were suspended mainly for disciplinary reasons, cutting school, cutting classes. These students didn't know (or care) about the function of school in the society or the various political reasons for not liking the schools. All they knew was that schools sucked and they wanted to keep away from them.

But this year students are wiser. A ten week teachers' strike woke them up to a lot of things happening around them. Where once students skipped school if they didn't like it, they began this year to talk about and take action designed to speed up taking over their schools. Community central and students' rights have become more important than cutting classes. And the man has responded accordingly. Not only has there been a change in the number of suspensions, there has been a change in the types of suspensions given out.

This year the suspensions have been mostly political

NEW YORK
HIGH SCHOOL
FREE PRESS
No. 7
New York

in nature, with administrators trying to keep the activists from their fellow students.

The Board of Education has specific rules regarding the process of suspending students. But, in the mad, fanatical attempt to suppress student and black community movements toward viable public education, the administrators of New York high schools have ignored even the unfair rules that they themselves established.

According to Board of Education Circular No. 16, dealing with the procedures to be used when suspending a student, no one but the principal of a school is empowered to suspend a student. Despite that rule, hundreds of students have been suspended this year by assistant principals and deans. In other cases the recommendations of teachers give them the right to suspend students too, with principals suspending students on the advice of teachers.

Even principals violate the rules supposedly set up to help the students. Students are not formally suspended until their parents are notified, but Ron Dicks, a Taft High School student suspended for giving out two copies of the Black Student Union newspaper, was forcibly ejected from the school when he asked that his parents be informed of his suspension.

Students are not supposed to be suspended for more than five days without a hearing in front of the district superintendent, but Paul Steiner and Jon Grell, students at the Bronx High School of Science, were suspended for over two weeks by principal Alexander Taffel. They finally received their hearing much later.

The basic purpose in suspending students is to isolate, from the rest of the student body, those students with ideas in opposition to those of the established order. Students are marked absent every day of their suspensions. They receive failing marks for all work missed while out. The addition of absences is one of the most damaging aspects of suspensions. If you consider that most suspensions last at least five days, and that a student is allowed only eighteen absences each semester, then you can see how a principal's suspension hinders a student's chances of promotion and/or graduation. Of course, that might be one of the purposes of suspensions.

The increase in the proportion of white students suspended this year is a direct result of the increased political activity in white middle class schools. Students have been suspended for handing out leaflets, distributing newspapers, and holding meetings.

Even when run "by the book," suspensions procedures are unfair to the student, denying him his basic constitutional rights. Students are not allowed to have lawyers present at suspension hearings. They also cannot cross-examine the people who testify against them. The student *is* nigger in these hearings, and in the finest American tradition, he is guilty until proven innocent.

Midwood High School in Queens was the scene of innumerable suspensions this year and last. Innumerable indeed! Innumerable and unaccountable, because the principal neglected to file reports of suspension with his district superintendent, as is required by the Board of Education. Midwood's principal remembered to file only three reports of suspension; Manhattan Vocational filed none. This, for the whole 1967–68 term.

Yet, it is known that no New York City school had so few suspensions last year. Thousands of "verbal" suspensions, with principals ordering students to leave the building, occur. These suspensions are never reported, and students are kept from classes without justification.

Suspended students unite! Together we can protect ourselves from the attacks. An alliance of students suspended for working to change the schools is necessary to halt the repression that is coming our way. The city has seen that suspensions, transfers, and failing report cards aren't enough to stop us. Lindsay has promised to arrest students who cause disorders in the schools and the Board of Education is training plainclothes cops for permanent assignment to "troubled" schools. We'll have to show them that that ain't enough to stop us either. ONWARD THE STRUGGLE! STUDENT POWER!!

FOLD THIS UP AND CARRY IT WITH YOU

FROM A H.S. STUDENT UNION LEAFLET *New York*

We're on the move in New York City. But the government is also moving—against us. The Black Panthers have been jailed, welfare demonstrators have been beaten up and high school students suspended. Arrests and harassment are increasing. Here are some basic rules for avoiding useless arrests and injuries and for handling it when you get busted.

COP-FRONTATION

Cops may stop you on the street even when you're not in a demonstration. They will question and frisk you. If you're alone, there is probably nothing you can do to stop them. You can, however, sometimes avoid a useless bust by acting respectful and giving innocuous answers to their questions instead of asserting your rights.

DON'T TALK TO INVESTIGATORS!

Local cops and the FBI may question you. Don't answer! You have a right to remain silent. Don't try to argue with them or outsmart them. You never know what use they can make of what you say and lying to them can be a crime. If it's too hard to refuse outright to talk, you can say, "I don't want to talk until I speak with my lawyer."

PREPARATION FOR A DEMONSTRATION

Dress for action: women should wear pants and no

OUR TIME IS NOW

earrings; wear shoes, not sandals; do not wear glasses unless absolutely necessary; wear a hat or a helmet and a heavy sweater to soften blows if it might be a rough demonstration.

If there is a possibility of tear gas and Mace: bring *plastic goggles* which can fit over glasses to protect your eyes from Mace and tear gas. Bring a *damp cloth* to cover your mouth and nose from tear gas. Cover your face with *vaseline* to protect yourself against Mace. Remove the vaseline as soon as you are Maced or you will get a slow burn.

Don't ever carry penknives or even a nail file to a demonstration; they can charge you with possession of a dangerous weapon.

Don't ever carry drugs to a demonstration.

Don't bring your address book; if you are busted, the cops will get the names of all your friends.

Carry the number of a lawyer or defense organization written on your arm or a piece of paper.

IN A DEMONSTRATION

Stay with a small group of friends and decide what to do together.

Demonstrations are infiltrated with plainclothes cops who often look like us. If you spot a cop, expose him to other people. Never accept a brick, spray paint, or a package with undisclosed contents from someone you don't know. If you've done something for which you might be arrested, don't think you haven't been seen just because there are no uniformed cops around; you might not want to hang around.

WHEN YOU'RE BUSTED

Don't try to talk the cop out of busting you or ask what the charges are. There is no chance of his releasing you and great chance that you will make admissions and get yourself and friends into trouble.

If there's no one around who knows you, shout out

your name so that someone in the crowd can call a lawyer.

Try to get the badge and radio-car number of the cop who busts you; notice the circumstances of the arrest and write them down as inconspicuously as possible. All this information may be useful during your trial.

IN CAPTIVITY

Especially if you are under twenty-one, your parents should come to the police station. They can be of great help in getting you released.

You have a right to make phone calls as soon as you get to the police station, and you should ask to do this. Often, however, they will not let you call for a while. First call a lawyer, then call a friend or relative who can come to your arraignment with cash for bail.

If a cop says, "There is an Attorney X on the phone, does he represent you?" you should answer "yes"; it means that someone has called a lawyer for you. The cops may be more cautious with you if they know you have a lawyer. You can always change lawyers later.

Only answer questions about name, address, age, occupation, and prior convictions. Give an address where there's someone who will say that you live there. Do not answer questions about drugs or about what you did. If the cops harass you, try to put them off but not antagonize them; say something like, "I don't want to talk until my lawyer gets here." DON'T TALK. DON'T TALK. DON'T TALK. DON'T TALK. DON'T TALK.

The cops have a right to search you once they arrest you, and they probably will.

You may be able to get a summons, like a traffic ticket; it allows you to go home immediately and requires your appearance in court the next day. If they don't mention it, ask, "Can't I get out on a summons?"

ARRAIGNMENT (for people sixteen and over)

After booking at the police station you will be taken

to the courthouse and put into a cell called the bullpen. Probably you will feel isolated and scared as you get dragged around from one place to another. It will all be easier if you talk to the other prisoners.

A probation officer will ask you questions in order to advise the judge whether to release you without bail. Sometimes his recommendation influences the judge; if you have nothing to hide you should answer the questions, although you don't have to.

Then you will go before the judge to hear your charge and have bail set. If you have no private attorney, ask the judge for a legal aid attorney. You can get your own lawyer after arraignment. If you are charged with a minor offense called a violation (disorderly conduct, loitering), you should plead "not guilty"; you can always change your plea later. If you are charged with a misdemeanor or a felony, you should enter no plea at all at this time.

HELPING YOUR FRIENDS

If you see someone arrested and you don't know his or her name, try to find it out. Then call a lawyer and tell him about the arrest and ask him to call the police station. Get as much cash as you can and take it to the arraignment. It is great to see friends in the courtroom.

Where the courts are located: Manhattan—100 Centre St. (City Hall or Canal St. subway); Brooklyn—120 Schermerhorn; Bronx—162nd St. and Washington Place; Queens—125-05 Queens Blvd.

If your friend was arrested before 3:30 in the afternoon or after 10:30 at night, he or she will be taken to Day Court in whatever borough the arrest occurred. If your friend was arrested between 3:30 in the afternoon and 10:30 at night, he or she will be taken to Night Court. (These hours are approximate.) The Manhattan Night Court is used for people arrested in Manhattan and the Bronx. The Brooklyn Night Court is used for people arrested in Brooklyn and Queens.

Lawyers: National Lawyers Guild: 962–5440; 227–0385; Emergency Civil Liberties Committee: 683–8120

Doctors: Medical Committee for Human Rights: 927–6073; 243–8686; 427–6499

High School Student Union: 799-2020

N.Y. Regional SDS: 674–8310

        The high school commune is the center for much of the organizing that goes on in New York City high schools. The students involved with it form programs and make demands constantly. The following article, "Troublemaker's Communique: 2," expresses the goals of the Student Union concerning the mobilization of New York City students:

TROUBLEMAKER'S COMMUNIQUE: 2

H.S. Committee

FROM AN H.S.
COMMUNE
LEAFLET
New York

        According to the newspapers, a small group of outsiders is responsible for the "disorders" in the schools. Talking about conspirators, outside agitators, and disruptive students allows the city government to ignore the real problems of a racist school system that has to be done away with. We, the students that must suffer through school every day, know that the only outside agitators in the schools are the police; that

OUR TIME IS NOW

the only disruptive influences in the schools are the irrelevant classes we must attend; that the only conspiracy is a conspiracy to brainwash us and to control our lives.

By creating a conspiracy in the high school movement, Mayor Lindsay wants to make it seem like there's a small group of people leading a larger group of weak-minded, impressionable students. And by arresting this small group (which is a very real possibility at this time), he thinks that the disorders will cease. What he doesn't know is that this is no part-time recreation of a bunch of hippy-yippie! extremists—it is the full-time commitment of every aware student in the New York City Public School System.

The strength of our movement and the strength of our politics is not measured by how many people we can turn out of school. Three kids can close down a school. But just closing a school doesn't change anything. For one day, we stand around in the sun for a while and talk. Then we all have to go back to school—back into the same cesspool we broke out of.

We have to realize that we are not going to get our demands by demonstrating. A rally at the Board of Education or a picket or march at a school isn't going to force the system to get the cops out, or to open up the colleges or the trade unions, or to give us the good jobs and decent housing we need. The principals aren't going to stop suspending or expelling students. We have to realize that our demands strike at the foundations of the school system. They aren't going to "give" us what we need—and we aren't playing around. We *need* the things that the student unions demand. We will not get these demands until we get our brothers and sisters together. Demonstrations are not an end. They are a tool that we can use to get our people together. We cannot measure our success by the numbers we turn out. We measure our success by the number of people we change.

By how many students learn what we are involved in, and become prepared to move to get what we want.

The demonstrations going on are important because a lot of people learned what the schools are all about, and why there are cops in the halls. At some schools the students demanded the "right" to sit on discipline committees or on student-faculty boards. Those demands can be met by the principals. That's because it is not a success to get to be on a pig committee: That's where the principals want us to be. And we don't want to organize principals or teachers. We want to organize ourselves—the students.

Our actions this spring are good and we can use them as a tool to get together and to organize. The groups that got together during the actions should see themselves as having a responsibility to all the students. We pulled people out supposedly to support the demands we believe are real. We have the responsibility of educating our brothers as to why these demands are real to us. We have to talk about what the demands mean as a whole program. And we have to help everybody learn why the demands will not and cannot be met in this society. We can use the *Free Press* and leaflets and films to start discussions. Everybody who is in a school where there was any kind of excitement last week should be rapping about what we are doing, why, and what we will have to do to survive in the future.

The media was quick to point out that, "the incidents involved white and black, boy and girl, students" (*The New York Times*), and this really got them upset. Because now, for the first time, the people can win. They've used racism for centuries to keep us split up. They make us think that our interests are different from the other guys. We're getting together now because we're beginning to realize that our enemy is the same: this SYSTEM. And we're going to fight it together: AS BROTHERS AND SISTERS—not in the bullshit way they use the words—really.

If our actions this spring really caused them to respond—and they are—by locking us up, busting our heads, and giving us bullshit concessions, it's only because of this. When black and white kids fought each other in Franklin Roosevelt, it didn't accomplish anything—the Man was glad. We really have to watch out what's said in the press, because they want this kind of thing to continue, they want us split and fighting among ourselves.

Organizationally, the Afro-American Students' Association, the Black Student Union, the Black High School Coalition, and the High School Student Union are working in close communication, on the local and city-wide level. While we must realize that the purpose of black student groups is to organize and educate black students, and that the purpose of white student groups is to organize and educate white students, we have to support each other in our actions and demands.

We're beginning to learn who our enemies are. You can't be neutral in this fight; you're either for us or against us; you're either part of the problem or part of the solution. We are learning who controls this country and we know it's not the people. The mass media is run by the ruling class—the directors of corporations, landowners, bankers, and the military people. Our fight is with them. When you are at war you don't tell your plans to the enemy. You don't tell them anything. Cops may be nice guys, but they follow orders from the Man. Reporters are the same. They're not hip to who it is they're helping by working for the TIMES, POST, LIFE, NBC, etc. REPORTERS ARE COPS! ACT ACCORDINGLY!

The fight we have begun is not going to be won this spring, nor is it going to be fought by high school students alone. The schools are not the only place we have to rebuild. GI's, poor people, workers fighting racist labor unions, college students, communities fighting to control their own hospitals, we are all in the same struggle. We should not think of what we are doing as only a high school fight but as part of a MOVEMENT. High school students are only high school kids for four years, but we have to live in this country for our whole life. We're going to have a lot of defeats, and some victories. They'll give us small things to keep us from demanding the real solutions. We have to remember that whatever is given to us can be taken back. What we are really engaged in is getting people together to get the POWER to give themselves what we need. ALL POWER TO THE PEOPLE! If we change one mind it's more of a victory than a thousand bullshit concessions.

The seriousness of the situation is of an importance that cannot be overstressed. When we reach the point where the Mayor of our city will purposely and willfully order judges to charge excessive bail for students arrested; when the spokesman for NYC's high school principals calls for the formation of work camps for "disruptive students," when plainclothes and uniformed pigs are allowed to walk in and out of the high schools, terrorizing and intimidating students, then we know the gravity of our situation. The power structure is out to get YOU and YOU and YOU if you're in favor of change in this society. We must recognize this and begin to act accordingly. We must be serious at all times, even if we are not solemn; we must be wary at all times, even if we are not paranoid.

YES, WE ARE THE CONSPIRACY, ALL 275,000 OF US.

WE DARE CONSPIRE TO BE FREE.

H.S. Commune

While I realize the strength of its rhetoric, I disagree with some of what is said in the "Troublemaker's Communique." I don't believe that

OUR TIME IS NOW

"the Man" was made happy, for instance, when black and white students fought each other at Franklin Roosevelt High School in New York. However, I do agree that black and white students should work together to accomplish each other's goals. I also don't believe that the high school students are working in the same "struggle" as the college students. However, I do believe that high school and college students aren't so far apart that they could never help each other. The "Troublemaker's Communique" is an appeal to student paranoia. It makes some good points, but, for the most part, it tries to unite students by setting up a common enemy for all of them. ("The Man" is the enemy. You must stop fighting each other and fight him.) It can be an effective way to mobilize, but I think it is a mistake. We must be honest with each other or the movement will fall apart.

This paranoid kind of organizing is most common in New York City. Some people might say that the New York students are more sophisticated and therefore more radical than the rest of the underground. I would disagree. The reason why New York students sometimes resort to paranoid rhetoric is that they have a much larger job to do than students in other schools. They have to mobilize more students, and, even more important, more different kinds of students. It is a tremendous job to try to get so many different kinds of people together. And although I don't like its methods that much, the High School Student Union has done a phenomenal job.

Most of the high school underground movement is not paranoid. High school revolutionaries tend to be less paranoid than college revolutionaries because they are younger and have experienced less opposition. They are often willing to bend over backwards to reach an agreement with the administration, as with the case of *Frox* mentioned earlier. (The *Frox* staff was willing to have a faculty advisor, agree to no obscenity and to having every article read by the principal before it was published, just so that they could legally distribute their uncensored paper on school grounds.) Most students involved with the underground seem to agree with the editor of *Mindfood*, of Pelham, New York, who urged me not to seek confrontation for the sake of publicity. As she put it: "Your purpose is to get your paper *read!*"

Even in New York City, students in the underground usually recognize their mistakes. The following article, which appeared in the *Weakly Reader*, is an example:

. . . WHILE IRVING SIMMERS
Eve Rosenhaft

WEAKLY
READER
No. 13
New York

The spring offensive has become little more than offensive. It has developed into something dangerous and frightening. In a period like ours—a revolutionary period—violence is to be expected; violence in the high schools is an understandable outgrowth of violence in the streets and universities. But I shudder at the thought of our accepting the kind of hysterical unreason that prevails today among high school students.

Where there is no peaceful recourse against an oppressive regime, violence is an acceptable—even necessary—means to an end. Assume that the New York City public school system constitutes an oppressive regime (even the best high schools operate under a kind of gently paternalistic repression). Then violence is, theoretically, a reasonable tactic. The questions to be considered now are whether the theory can effectively be applied to the existing situation—i.e., will violence work in the city schools? And if so, how is that violence to be implemented, and what will it lead to? In other words, what's your plan, Brother?

The answer has been, up to now, "Don't ask stupid questions. Can't you see I'm busy?" Sure, radicals have been able to find excuses for violence: The non-negotiable demands are presented—along with a dazzling, ingenuous promise that if the demands are met, another issue will be found. This indicates that the present activity in the high school is seemingly without a constructive goal.

Quite the contrary. There is a prevailing attitude today that the job of the socially concerned student is to burn down the schools. A little thoughtful consideration will reveal that to destroy the schools (or the welfare centers or the hospitals) without replacing them would be to work a criminal hardship on this city.

In fact, this is a manifestation of the confused focus which handicaps radical youth today. Students have consistently failed to identify the enemy. In the universities, young people enraged at society attack administrators, who in the larger context are powerless. And in the high schools, students misdirect their rage at the schools themselves. Thus, we demand an end to the high school tracking system, which, when effective, is the only way the high school can train children intellectually crippled in ghetto schools. The answer to Southern school segregation was not to destroy the Southern schools. Even where the tracking system is used to perpetuate racial segregation under one roof, the answer is not to abolish the entire system. When we are reasonably enough refused in our demands for even more impotent high schools, we begin making Molotov cocktails.

Strike. But strike at the roots of the problems, not the branches. Violence is an effective means in the schools, if the end is the destruction of the high schools in New York City. But there can be no meaningful revolution in public education if there are no schools left.

A STUDENT RAPS ABOUT STUDENT POWER

Quickly gaining momentum, swept along by the forces of the Free Speech Movement and civil rights agitation, is the urgent movement for Student Power. For the first time in history, the under-25

SANSCU-
LOTTES
No. 28
Bronx, New York

FIVE

Student Power

population, students for the most part, comprises a majority in this nation. Yet, the initiative to explore new ideas with an open mind, so vital to a dynamic society, is severely inhibited by a hypocritical educational structure that, on one hand, professes to train students to think for themselves, while in fact it maintains restrictions on our minds, voices, and lives. It is this point that is the key to the need for student power.

First, it is important to analyze the structure we are dealing with. Public education has traditionally played the role of apologist for the system that fosters it. It serves in a capacity similar to that of the mass media: that is, to present such a picture of society that the youth will mature into passively acquiescing adult members. The social role played by the educational structure is directly related to the society's need to establish authority and authority figures. It is important to realize that all of the policies, decisions, and actions of the Board of Education are related to these roles. The Board's power is great and for the most part very effective with the students, who are under its control six hours a day, five days a week. Curriculum, study materials, and activities are geared to maintain this government's political control, and the teacher, instead of becoming an integral part of classroom knowledge-probing, is placed above the students, and often above the vital learning process, by the authority he represents and wields. The voice of neither the student nor his parents is heard in determining a major aspect of his youth that will affect his attitudes and ideas for the remainder of his life.

Keeping in mind the structure within which we must work (for now, at least), let us examine some specific grievances and proposals for constructive student power. First, there are several significant constitutional issues that have arisen. Guarantees of free speech, a free press, the right to petition, the right to assemble, and the right to due process are denied students within the confines of the school. The justification offered by the authorities amounts to the theory "in loco parentis" which states that the school administration must take the place of the parents for the duration of the school day. The rationality of this theory is severely dented when one realizes that freedom inspires responsibility to insure that freedom; if students were given the right to be responsible for themselves, necessity would insure that they accepted that responsibility.

Students should be allowed, therefore, to form groups and meet on campus, to distribute and/or sell printed matter, and to circulate and present petitions. Staff positions on the school papers (at least two in order to allow for editorial disagreement) should be open to every student, and editorial policy should be determined by a majority of the staff. Any faculty advisor should serve merely as advisor, with no veto or censor powers. Furthermore, to insure fair and impartial disciplinary actions, an elected student-faculty-administration board of discipline should be established, with each member having an equal vote. At the same time, I would hope that the outdated regulations now in effect (the cause of most disciplinary actions), would be subject to radical revision, especially those regulations that serve no constructive purpose, but are merely established to maintain the authority of the faculty and administration in preparation for the many authority figures of the society. Restrictions on dress and attire should be abolished, and elimination of present "security regulations," such as out of building and late passes, hallway passes, and absence notes, should be examined. Serious consideration, too, should be given to the elimination of the dominating kindergarten aura in the city's high schools, by transforming the present class requirements from mandatory to, in many classes, a more lenient attendance policy, with a final exam of pass-fail status. This proposal reflects a reaction against two prevailing characteristics of student life: one, that attendance is a major criterion for grading in all subjects, and two, that grading itself is on a viciously competitive basis. These two are interrelated to the extent that attendance becomes part of that overwhelming pressure for a high numerical grade. This pressure induces memorization, rather than true education. A pass-fail system, therefore, would relieve the student of his burden of grade-pressures and at the same time would not pretend to arbitrarily graph a student's mind on a 0 to 100 scale. High school classes today often turn out to be only study or reading sessions, or homework review sessions. Attendance in that type of class may not be necessary for grasping the subject itself. Therefore, mandatory attendance in any one class should be limited to an established minimum for credit consideration (taking into consideration the type of class and related requirements). Absences from the class, including absences from the school altogether, should not be taken into account until they transcend the minimum attendance requirement for that class. Recalling the structure of a pass-fail system, it's obvious that "excessive" absences do not necessitate a fail grade, but may raise questions as to the validity of an unqualified pass grade.

The question of curriculum and its control arises now amidst much controversy. At this point, control of courses and graduation requirements rests in the hands of the State Board of Regents, the Board of Education, and, to a lesser degree, the local school. This total separation of curriculum determination from those most affected by it is the major aspect of all of the problems plaguing today's schools. Relevance of studies to the student's life is of prime importance to his educational experience. The student himself should have the right to make his own choice of courses from the optionals, beyond the course requirements established by a community-faculty board.

The basis of an educational experience is the curriculum it offers. By decentralizing the structure, giving a voice to those most affected, and opening the doors for more relevant study, the student's will to probe and absorb will be allowed, for once, to increase, and the educational level of this nation may at last rise to a point rivaling the progressive and very successful European and private schools.

Student Power, then, is a general term encompassing many aspects of high school life. It is time that the student's voice is heard and his rights guaranteed, his mind opened and his life free from the educational structure that now tenaciously retains the past. The student power movement is working and pushing toward these goals, and its urgency is only heightened by the state of our affairs in the world today.

Sansculottes has just summed up what student power is all about. Simply stated, student power involves a complete change in the role that the student plays in his school. It means that students are given real authority to change their school.

Right now—to repeat myself—the greatest obstacle in the way of student power is adults' fear. Here is where I notice some paranoia on the part of the administrations. Administrators have told me that they are afraid to give students more authority in school because if the students used this power to change the school in a way that doesn't suit the parents, the parents would come down upon the administration. These administrators have been proven right. The Mahwah *Oracle* case is an example of parents using their power to stop student power. The transcript of the Board of Education meeting that appears in Chapter 2 shows just how outspoken some of these parents can get. But these parents are not all parents. My parents, for example, agreed with me that censorship of the school paper by the administration should be ended. But because they did not make nasty phone calls to the principal's office, he paid more attention to the parents who did make such calls.

My parents didn't make nasty calls to the principal because they believed that fighting censorship of the paper that I was editing was my concern. If I wanted them to make these calls, they probably would have, but I agreed with them that it was my fight. I wish more parents thought the same way as mine. After all, isn't the school supposed to be serving the students, not the parents? Parents may argue that high school students aren't mature enough to have authority in their school. But hasn't the initiative that the students have shown in the underground proven otherwise?

The obvious place to begin to give power to students is in the Student Council. The administration can begin by changing the "toy" government that students play with into a real government with which they can really take action and learn. Now, the only democratic principle that students get to practice is electing their representatives. But these representatives have no working power, so what is the point of electing them? They can talk with the administration, but not really better than any other student. They can vote on some change, and if the principal agrees with it and decides not to use his all-powerful veto, the change will be passed. But that's another way of saying that the Student Council can do anything the principal wants them to. The Student Council can also initiate dances and cookie sales without too much interference from the administration. Big deal. Obviously, many changes must be made.

In the following article, some of those changes are discussed.

TOWARD A DEMOCRATIC STUDENT GOVERNMENT
John Koskinen, Richard Shadden, and Stuart Steffan

MINSTREL
Vol. II, No. 1
Waukegan,
Illinois

It has been quite obvious for some time that Student Council has not given experience and efficiency in the practice of democracy nor is it able to practice democracy. The Dress Code Committee's report was the latest indication of its failure to do so. The Student Council opposed the student's report and favored the administration's view. It is clear, despite all pretenses to the contrary, Student Council is not a democracy: It is a puppet government.

There is a reason for everything. The reason Student Council operates as a puppet government is that it is structured like a puppet government. In order to remedy the situation, the Fourth Estate proposes the following major changes in order for Student Council to become a democratic organization.

1. The most obvious step to take would be elimination of the administration's absolute veto. Allow the council to override an administration veto by ⅔ majority vote.

2. Modify the sponsor's role to a silent observer, nothing more. This would put greater responsibility on the representatives and take away an omnipresent representative of the administration.

3. Reform the election procedures. Replace the present petition for office with a petition consisting of the candidate's name, the office he seeks, and 100 student signatures. After he files this completed petition he would be placed on the primary ballot. The administration or faculty would thereby have no say in candidates.

Presently, in order to run for office, a candidate must seek approval from the Assistant Principal, Student Council Sponsor, Class Counselor, Student Council President or Vice-President, and the candidate's teachers. The students, with the exception of one, have no say in candidates that will be placed on the primary ballot. The administration, on the other hand, has the opportunity to select only those favorable to their viewpoint.

Eliminate grade average as a qualification for office. Presently, one must have a 2.0 average to run for office, thereby excluding approximately one half of the student body.

The elections would be held in the fall rather than in the spring. Thereby, we would include the enthusiasm of the incoming freshman class, also giving them a say in who represents them and excluding the apathy of the outgoing seniors.

Results of the primary election and the final election would be published rather than kept secret and merely announcing the winner. Allow the candidate to request a recount.

Do not allow Student Council to supervise the election. Have election judges supervise the election. Election judges would be students. Student or class council members would not be eligible to be election judges. Also, all poll watchers.

4. In order to give practice in democracy it is essential that we have a system of appeals for those accused of violating regulation. Ergo, we suggest the following Student-Faculty Court:

The student-faculty court would consist of four members of the faculty and three members of the student body. One of the four faculty members would be the student council sponsor. The other three would be elected by the faculty. The student judges would be elected by the same process as the student council members. There would be no class distinction on eligibility.

It would be an appellate court. It would give the students a recourse to unreasonable administrative action. A student would fill out a necessary form indicating his reason for appeal and the administrative decision he wishes to appeal. Appeals can be denied by the court, if the court feels the case does not warrant a hearing. Suspensions and expulsions are given automatic appeals and hearings because of their severity.

With the system we have outlined above, we feel we can achieve a student democracy and increased student participation.

The next most obvious place to give students power is on the school newspaper. Censorship by the administration must be eliminated. This again brings up the question of parent power vs. student power. And again, I think that the students can handle the power. I doubt that a significant number of parents would ever object to a liberalized overground paper.

Freedom of speech, of course, was the kind of student power that I worked hardest for. This power can be taken, as I have said before, by going underground. Still, I don't think the overground press should be ignored.

The following article was printed alongside of the letter that I wrote to my principal asking him to give students the authority to censor their own paper. The article encourages students to take freedom of speech through the overground and the underground.

STOP CENSORSHIP

SMUFF
Vol. I, No. 2
Hackensack,
New Jersey

On the following page, page 7, is a letter to the administration from John Birmingham. It requests that the power of censorship of the Voice be moved from the administration to a democratic editorial board. The administration has refused this request and said that it can not foresee a time when the administration will no longer censor the Voice.

Yet despite this firm stand on censorship, apparently the administration fears neither obscenity nor criticism, only controversy. This was grounds for censorship of part of a budget-cut editorial and drawn-out debates over several other articles. But who is really going to be offended by such controversy? Won't it be the adults of the Hackensack community, some of the students' parents, the ones who might call our school to complain about the "subversive" literature that might be put into the Voice? And so, the Voice, supposedly a student newspaper, must act to maintain good public relations between the administration and the community.

As long as the Voice is censored by the administration, its staff functions solely as a public relations manager for the H.H.S. administration. This is an exploitation of students. It is not as serious an exploitation as it would be if the Voice staff were obliged to spend their spare time scrubbing the floors of the administrative offices, nevertheless . . .

What is censored is irrelevant. Censorship by the administration says that the students must not express their opinions frankly in the Voice. It says that the Voice editorial board must not have the learning experience of being responsible for what is printed in their own newspaper.

The administration is presently immovable on this subject. That means that *you*, as a student, can know where the administration is and can walk around it. Here are two ways to begin with:

1. Petition. Work through Smuff Student Coalition (see page 3) and through the Student Council. Talk with your representative. See if the Student Council has any meaningful power.

2. Express your opinions anyway. Write for the Voice. Write for *Smuff*. If the Voice cannot accept your article, *Smuff* can.

Start the inevitable; stop censorship.

Probably the most dramatic power that students can use today is the law. If a student's rights are violated, he can take his high school administration to court. One girl at a meeting about censorship at the Columbia Scholastic Press Association Convention said that she and the American Civil Liberties Union were suing her school's principal for censoring her school's newspaper. In the case of the *Oracle* in Mahwah, New Jersey, the editors are suing their school board of education for the right to distribute their paper on school grounds.

Other examples follow:

MINER AND ACLU TO SUE DISTRICT #1

Bruce Merrick, Catalina sophomore, was suspended for three weeks for passing out *Mine* in his P.E. class and is now planning to sue the district. He has the backing of the ACLU, and is planning to file within a month.

MINE
No. 8
Tuscon,
Arizona

Bruce is looking for other students who would like to file a joint suit. This would entail giving a testimonial to the effect that you would have passed out literature if you hadn't been afraid of getting suspended. The only group now actively supporting Bruce is the ACLU, so he needs your help. Any Catalina student who would like to testify should get in touch with Bruce.

Bruce was suspended while passing out *Mine* on campus on April 21. He made two more trips back to school, April 29 and May 1, to obtain the charge against him in writing, which, when he finally got it, was "distributing off-campus literature on campus." He was suspended until he promised not to pass out material and submit to the rules of the school. Bruce promised pending a law suit, and was allowed back in school May 15.

GIRL IN STUYVESANT?

WEAKLY
READER,
No. 10
New York

"The morals of Stuyvesant High School are being corrupted!" cried Clifton D. Wellman III, Secretary of the Stuyvesant G.O. in anguish. The news that a girl was trying to get into the all-boy Stuyvesant was received with less chagrin (in fact, with visible pleasure) by most other Stuyvesant students. A few days after the first report concerning her audacious exploits in *The New York Times* of January 21, International Alice Day was proclaimed, and students celebrated by taking over the West Cafeteria, dubbing it Alice's Restaurant, and dissipating with popcorn, trumpets, harmonicas, and balloons.

The Girl is Alice de Rivera, a beautiful fourteen-year-old from Brooklyn's fashionable Cobble Hill. Now a freshman at John Jay High, she hopes to transfer for her sophomore year at Stuyvesant. Originally denied, she was finally allowed to take the Stuyvesant entrance examination at Bronx High School of Science on January 23. If she passes, the New York State Supreme Court will rule on her admission on February 26. Alice is beautiful and intelligent. She maintains an all-round average in the mid-90's. She is active in radical politics, edits the inchoate underground newspaper at John Jay, *The Streetfighter,* and delivers her brother's morning paper route when he can't make it.

Alice was interviewed at the SDS Regional Office by Toby B. Mamis of the *New York Herald Tribune* and Honest Bob Singer of the *Weakly Reader:*

WEAKLY READER: How did officialdom respond to you?
ALICE: The school refused me because I'm a girl. The

Board of Education refused because of something called Circular 13, which prohibits transfer into a specialized high school. They're not using that excuse any more. The court said I could take the test at Bronx Science.

HERALD TRIBUNE: Why Bronx Science?

A: So there wouldn't be any trouble at Stuyvesant—saved face for the Board of Education.

WR: What will you do if you pass the test and are denied admission?

A: We'll take the case as far as the Supreme Court.

WR: Are any other girls trying to get into Stuyvesant?

A: No, but some others will try if I'm refused because I'm only one.

WR: Do you anticipate any problems with your possible new classfellows?

A: No.

WR: Teachers?

A: I hope not.

WR: Facilities. You know, bathrooms and all that.

A: I'm very optimistic.

WR: Are you going to demand special shops when you get in—cooking, etc.?

A: No, I'd like to learn printing.

HT: Why?

A: I want to put out a newspaper.

HT: Do you think you'll have a disruptive effect at Stuyvesant?

A: I intend to be disruptive not with my presence, but with my ideas.

WR: Will you join the G.O. and be active in G.O. politics?

A: What do you think?

WR: You think it's *&%#$.

A: Yes, awfully, I'd like to teach myself.

HT: What would you teach yourself?

A: Not what the System wants to teach me.

WR: Do you think that the present curricula are one-dimensional—that is, designed to opt the intellectual elite of which Stuyvesant High School is composed into the technocracy of the advance capitalist society?

A: Uh, yes.

HT: Do you hang around with hip kids? Where will you make your friends at Stuyvesant?

A: All over the place.

HT: In the bathrooms?

A: Sure, in the bathrooms.

HT: What does your social life consist of?

A: I meet people through political action.

WR: What do you read?

A: Books.

WR: Are there any books you think we should all read?

A: *Nigger*, Dick Gregory's autobiography.

WR: Whom did you support for the Presidency?

A: Gregory.

WR: What kind of music do you like?

A: Rock: the Doors, Jimi Hendrix, the Rolling Stones.

WR: What do you think of graffitti on school walls?

A: It's beautiful.

WR: If you're admitted to Stuyvesant, and the administration implemented a dress code, would you defy it? Wear mini-skirts, pants, run naked?

A: Whatever I felt like.

ALICE IN WONDERLAND
Toby Mamis

WEAKLY
READER
No. 13
New York
On Friday, May 2, at the offices of the Emergency Civil Liberties Committee, a "victory" was announced. Alice de Rivera, the fourteen-year-old female student at John Jay High School who had filed suit for admission to Stuyvesant, had been offered an

out-of-court settlement by the Board of Education. In effect, the settlement meant that the Board was willing to allow Alice to attend Stuyvesant in the fall of 1969. It did not specifically allow for application to other single-sex schools in the city. Washington Irving, Clinton, Boys High, Hunter, Brooklyn Tech, the list goes on and on.

While Alice's admission is an important first victory, we must now push for immediate (fall 1969) full and meaningful coeducation of Stuyvesant and all other single-sex schools. We must demand the admission of black and Puerto Rican girls (as well as many more black and Puerto Rican male students) to insure a balance close to that of the city-wide student population. 52.2 per cent of the city's school students are "non-white."

Back where I began: Alice was very happy that she had won. She said that it was a victory in the struggle against the Board of Education, and for Women's Liberation. An active member of the New York High School Student Union, she has been working for the spring offensive in her Brooklyn neighborhood and at John Jay.

Among the types of student power, some must be taken (as with freedom of speech), and some must be given to the student by the school (as with democratic power for the Student Council). Violence comes somewhere in between the two. The student is using his own power when he is violent; nobody gives him the violence. But he is not really taking anything either. All he is left with is violence and a lot of angry people.

However, some of the muscle that has been most recognized by adults has been because of violence. The high school students in New York City, for example, have received much press coverage because they have employed violence. The mass media press realizes how large the High School Student Union is because the Student Union has, according to the press, been behind much of the violence in New York high schools.

The Student Union cannot really claim credit for all this violence. For the most part, violence in the high schools is not organized or initiated by the underground. It is not usually organized by anyone. The violence is usually an expression of justifiable frustration and anger on the part of the students.

In one case in particular, however, the Student Union, along with the Black Student Union and the Afro-American Students' Association, was behind violence. The date was April 21, 1969, and the violence was meant to enforce the demands of the students. It was planned and organized violence, something that doesn't appeal to me personally. The style was too SDS-like. It did not really represent the high school underground movement on the whole, but it was what was happening in New York, so it was important.

The disruptions that occurred in New York high schools between April 21 and May 19 did not have a marked effect on the high school underground, but they did show the city just how much muscle the New York City high school underground had acquired. The demands weren't met. But lots of fires were started.

The following articles give the stories of these disruptions—before and after.

SPRING OFFENSIVE

NEW YORK
HIGH SCHOOL
FREE PRESS
No. 7
New York

We've all been shit upon in one way or another. But what did we do about it? Some of us dropped out. Others tore up bathrooms and desks and broke windows to tell them how we see the schools. I heard about a couple of Molotovs going off at Brooklyn Tech. Most of the kids still in the school get out of it by using dope. Scag, coke, grass and hash are all over the halls. Then the teachers' strike showed us how to really fuck up the schools. The teachers went out together and closed down the schools. The city called it a "crisis." While they were at home or on picket lines we took the schools. We learned what it meant to move as a group. The student unions and the black groups all over the city went into the schools and ran them themselves. We know what it is to move against the school system. But we've always done it as individuals. As loners. Troublemakers who were considered anti-social. This year we did it together.

But there's not much you can do against the schools alone. Not much at all. There are thousands of us who are down to fight. But fighting alone hasn't done shit towards changing the schools. Last year there were twelve thousand suspensions. Twelve thousand kids had to bring their parents in to see the principal. Twelve thousand of us had to hassle with the dean or the principal and sit there while he told us that we ought to drop out and get a job—we're just not fit for school. Or told to "talk" to our guidance counselors. Like we were crazy. Damn, we know that it's these schools and our parents that are crazy, not us. But what could we do about it? Not a thing. Some kids put out papers, to let us know that the schools suck—and they got suspended for telling us what we know already. A couple of kids got lawyers to defend them—and they won, but so what. When they went back to school and acted alive again, they were suspended again, and had to do it all over. No change, just more hassles. And that's just suspensions. How many brothers and sisters were transferred out of their schools or districts because some teacher or administrator wanted to get rid of them? At Brandeis, the principal decided that he wanted a smaller student body. So he kicked out all the "troublemakers" he could. If you were over seventeen you could be kicked out for cutting a couple of classes, or for being a "nuisance" to teachers. They throw us out. Every kid in the school system catches shit. We all know that. Not a single kid reading this paper is learning what he could in school. Not a single one of us is going to be able to choose what he wants to do after high school. Not one of us learns the skills needed to get a good job; most of us won't even get into college. Anyone who loses his program card can be picked up for trespassing. Everyone has to sit through the same bullshit courses, the same boring classes. We are all treated like dirt by teachers who think that being a teacher gives them some sort of super power.

Everyone's been fucked over by the schools, but who catches the worst shit? The "troublemakers." The ones who cut classes because they're boring and meaningless. Those kids who told the teachers what we all really think of them. Those who are always "hanging around" in the halls, trying to get our brothers together. The ones who opened the schools in the fall, and the ones who closed them down in the winter. Anyone who passes out a leaflet, or sells the *Free Press*. The militants, radicals, bad cats, troublemakers, organizers, agitators. We're all being pushed around like we're babies who

can't do shit to fight back. But the students are really
the most powerful people in the schools. We're the ones
that are ready to fight for what we should have. For what
we want.

What we learned this year is that it's just not enough
to be bad. We've got to be together. Bad cats get their
heads kicked. Union members fought together and pro-
tected each other's heads. We have to build unions.
Unions aren't bullshit organizations that give orders or
that get "social functions" together. Basketball games
and school dances are not what student unions will be
about. And neither is sitting in offices, or monthly dues.
Student unions are the banding together of all "troublemakers" and would-be "troublemakers" in schools. They
help us keep on fighting for what we want, without
getting screwed by the system. The High School Student Union, and The Black Student Union, and The
Afro-American Students' Association (and any other
groups like them) have to be built in every school. We
can't afford to say that unions and politics are just for
the middle class kids, or for the hippies, or for the militants, revolutionaries, radicals, or blacks. Every kid in
the schools gets shit. And those of us who fight against
that have to get together, or we're going to be squashed.

This spring we have a program to get together around.
There's going to be a lot happening in the city. In
Eastern District High School the students are already
in the streets. At Lincoln Hospital the community and
the community workers have taken the hospital for the
community and are ready to fight to keep it. There were
five fires set at Brooklyn Tech High School. There have
been anti-social riots at Canarsie and Jackson. Welfare
rights groups are getting together for a spring offensive.
That was during winter. The temperature's going up
inside. The temperature's going up outside. Last year
25 per cent of us were absent from school every day. Six
years ago there were only 9 per cent absent each day.

This spring there may be more people outside the schools than inside. We have got to make sure that when we're "absent from school" this spring that we're not just wasting time and ending up screwed by the schools again. We want to use that time to make damn sure that next fall we're not in the same lousy position we're in now:

This spring we're going to begin the fight to make the buildings they call schools useful.

WE DEMAND:

1. NO MORE SUSPENSIONS, no involuntary transfers, no exclusion from classes, no detention, no discharges, no harassment of students. All the forms of discipline peculiar to schools are oppressive. They don't protect us; they protect a racist, oppressive school system.

2. NO COPS IN SCHOOLS. There are cops in every high school in the city. We want them out. No undercover agents or informers in the schools.

3. NO PROGRAM CARDS. No hall checks, lunchroom checks, bathroom passes. The schools are there for us to use. The teachers have no right to tell us where we can or cannot go in the schools.

4. AN END TO GENERAL AND COMMERCIAL DIPLOMAS. The schools are made to separate us. They take white, middle class kids and put them into the IGC [intellectually gifted children] classes and SP [special progress] classes in grade and junior high school. Then in high school the white middle and upper class kids are put into "academic" courses. The black and Latin students, and the poor whites, are put into general and commercial courses. They say that we have freedom to choose which we're in, but that's bullshit. Students in the academic courses are encouraged to go into general courses, but the reverse never happens. Many students are put into general courses without being told. Others are told by their grade advisers that the general course is easier,

and just as good for a student who "isn't capable" of going to college. A general diploma is a ticket to the army. Nothing else. In the commercial and vocational courses students are trained for jobs that don't exist any more. Nearly every student graduating from vocational school was put into a job after he graduated. Only one in ten was able to keep it. That's about how well they train us. When we get out of high school the good jobs are going to require college training. And we all want to be able to get those jobs. We all want the same diploma to have the same chance.

A high school diploma doesn't mean anything unless we can get somewhere with it, so we demand as well:

5. OPEN ADMISSIONS TO COLLEGE. A college education free for everyone, and support for all students who need it through college. Columbia University, New York University, the City University, the community colleges, New York State University, and all other colleges in New York must open up to any high school graduate who wants in. Let them take money out of the armed forces to build enough facilities to give every one of us a place in college. Students on all campuses will fight together with us in the spring. The colleges have always been to educate the elite and leave the rest of us with lousy jobs and low wages. No more middle class. We all want to get good jobs and enough money to live.

6. We demand that there be a JOB AND DECENT HOUSING AVAILABLE for every high school student who drops out or graduates and doesn't want to go to college. Our people desperately need more and better housing, food, transportation, education. There is a labor shortage in all of these areas. And still we can't find jobs when we have to. We can't find jobs because the people who run the big businesses and the trade unions in this city don't think it's profitable for them.

Well, they don't have to live in our communities and they don't have to work for a living. Let them be unemployed and let us go to work at decent wages to build our communities up.

7. NO MILITARY RECRUITMENT IN SCHOOLS. The army is not a substitute for a good job. We want no military assemblies, no names to the draft boards, no army recruiters in the schools, an end to the draft. All of us that can't get jobs or can't get away from our parents but we can "join the army; see the world; learn a skill." Bullshit. The only part of the world you'll see in the army is basic training camp and Vietnam. The only skill you can learn is how to survive in a jungle war, against our brothers and sisters of Vietnam. When you get back from the army, you still have to find a job on a job market that doesn't have room for us. The war we have to fight is here, for good jobs, housing, education and an end to racism. Not one of us can afford to be shot at in Vietnam for the rich.

8. We demand BLACK AND LATIN DEPARTMENTS, controlled by the students. Departments must be established, controlled by the Black and Latin students to eliminate racism in the textbooks, in the teaching, in discipline.

There must be courses in Black and Latin history and culture set up in every school in the city. Black and Latin students must have the power to root out the racism that is forced on us.

9. COMMUNITY CONTROL of the schools and all other public facilities. That's what it's all about. The communities of this nation must take control of their own destinies. We must have power over the distribution of our own labor and money. We must control our schools, hospitals, police, welfare, and transportation. We are just as much a part of our communities as our parents. We must unite with them to take for the people the things that we and our parents have built up and paid for. We must control our own education. That education must serve the needs and wants of our

community, not some rich men at the board or the Mayor's office. "We want the world, and we want it now!"

10. POWER. We want student power. The only way that students can gain power over their own lives is to organize. Therefore we demand the right to get ourselves together for our own needs. This means: the right to leaflet, the right to have assemblies, real student government, the right to have newspapers and literature of our own, the right to have politics and ideology and political action in our own interests in the schools or for distributing leaflets, or for smoking in the halls. We've been busted and alone for talking back or for being against the UFT and the principals. Everything we have been busted for is important—to us. Each rule must be gotten rid of, as well as each racist teacher, each lousy textbook, each bad program, each obstacle to college admissions. Each one has to go. But we can only get rid of each one by getting rid of them all. If some kids in Seward Park go down to get rid of the general diploma and nobody else in the city is ready to go down with them, then they can't win. The principal will appoint a student-faculty committee, and transfer the "troublemakers" and that will be that. But the fight is not at Seward Park alone. There are students at every school in the city fighting against the schools. Even if for you that means fighting for Black and Latin courses or open admissions to college, we are still in the same fight as the Seward Park students. When the principal at Seward Park says no to their demands he is not saying no to the students of Seward, he is saying no to every student in the city. We must be prepared to support the struggles of high school students on every issue, in every school. If we support each other, we can win. If we only support ourselves, we will be fucked over like we never have been fucked before. The demands above are being made by the High School Student Union. The

High School Student Union is pulling together all students who are fighting against the school system. We will defend each other when the need arises. The brothers and sisters in the Bronx will be working together; in upper Manhattan, lower Manhattan, eastern Queens, western Queens, Brooklyn. Groups of five to ten schools will be going down together when it gets warmer. We will be moving directly against the source of our oppression. We will move directly, and we will move together.

The black students have declared April 21 as the day when we begin to move. The High School Students will stand by their black brothers and sisters. They will move their own groups to support the black students' movement and to take what the white students need for their community. We will use the spring actions to build strong groups in the schools that can move together, and a strong city-wide union that will bring us together for mutual defense.

The *High School Free Press* is being distributed in forty-seven high schools. Students who want to get it out where it is not yet available will be able to get copies. The *Free Press* will keep us aware of what is happening to our brothers and sisters around the city as they go out in the spring. The *Free Press* will also print as many leaflets as our organizations need to build and educate. All student groups that are moving against the repression we suffer can have material printed by the *Free Press*: 799–2020.

The Student Union will bring its people to support the actions of all students in the city. Students at any school can get in touch with the "troublemakers," black or white, at the schools near them through the Central Communications office: 799–2020.

Newsreel films are available through the Central Communications office.

LAWYERS and legal advice are available at Central Communications: 799–2020.

There will be leaflets printed around each of the demands. There will be posters along with the leaflets. These too will be available from Central Communications.

The Central Communications office will serve to keep us in touch with one another, and to print for us what we need to work with. They will make available to students at each school the contacts we need to become effective and to support and defend each other in our struggle. It is not an organization. It is established to help all us troublemakers build the organizations we want.

FROM APRIL 21 TO MAY 19 IS OUR MONTH! THE STREETS, THE SCHOOLS, THE COMMUNITIES ARE ALL OURS, WE'RE GOING TO TAKE THEM BACK!

POWER

The NY High School Student Union, the Black High School Student Coalition, the Afro-American Students Association, and the Black Student Unions called for disruptions in the city's schools from April 21 through May 19 to back up demands presented to the administrations of various schools and to the Board of Education.

NEW YORK HERALD TRIBUNE
No. 5
New York

They started right on schedule, and are still going on.

Van Buren—300 members of the BSU took over the cafeteria and the auditorium. A few fires and no arrests.

Walton—1,000 kids join a group of Clinton students. Three arrested.

Clinton—500 kids walked out and set fire to the basement. Then they went all over the neighborhood doing things.

Erasmus—A peaceful demonstration outside the school became a melee when the cops charged the gathering. At the same time, a few fires and bombs went off in the school. As the school was closed immediately, several hundred students joined the demonstrators and engaged in a real live street battle with the cops for a few hours. About twenty-five arrested, with several injuries. The next day, a new battle in which another thirty were busted. In the middle of the battle, the kids held a small restaurant as a first-aid station.

Springfield Gardens—Three students and a dean arrested after the cops charged a peaceful demonstration. Two days later, the students held the auditorium in support of their demands.

Tilden—When the principal of the school refused to let Les Campbell speak, the students took to the streets. After fires appeared, the school was closed.

Jackson—Seventeen kids arrested when the students take the auditorium and the cafeteria, and 1,500 of their supporters walk out of school.

Brooklyn Tech—300 Black students took over the auditorium and presented their demands to the administration.

Jefferson—School evacuated as a fire starts early in the morning. 400 kids meet with the principal in the auditorium to discuss "non-negotiable" demands.

Julia Richman—A fire in the basement closed the school early one day.

Eastern District—Vandals set fire to the records in the offices and swept through the school.

Teddy Roosevelt—Students burned an American flag, and went on a rampage throughout the school.

Westinghouse Vocational—150 students denied entrance after arriving late try and break through locked doors. After failure, they went on a rampage in the immediate vicinity.

Bronx Science—The students occupied the offices for a brief time, causing confusion.

Bushwick, Lincoln, and Morris also reported fires and rallies. At Canarsie, the black students took over the auditorium.

By the Staff, with the help of LNS and Howie Swerdloff and all the high school students in the streets, and, of course, the educational system, the cause for all this activity.

I repeat: The violence that occurred in New York does not represent the high school underground as a whole. However, since it is part of the movement, it must be represented.

My biggest objection to these actions is that it shows that some high school students are making some of the same mistakes as the SDS. And that was something I'd hoped to disprove completely. The following article expresses *Smuff*'s editorial stand on the SDS. (And we are not the only ones in the underground who feel this way.)

A NEED FOR CHANGE IN STUDENT RADICALISM

An immediate change must take place within the structures of organized student radicalism. And if the change does not come, radicalism will fall.

SMUFF
Vol. I, No. 1
Hackensack,
New Jersey

Organized radicalism hit a high point last spring with the SDS. The students had a good cause—to stop Columbia University from building a gym in Morningside Park and to return the park to its West Harlem community. Columbia had previously ignored its duties to the West Harlem community in which it is centered, so the righteousness of the students' cause was emphasized.

Since the student demonstrations were successful (Columbia stopped the construction of the gym), students have gained political power. And the SDS has gained strength.

But now, the SDS and other radical organizations have changed their style. The new style is typified by pointless violence. Recently, for example, two SDS members beat up a Columbia professor with a club. There was no difference between this action and the actions committed by the Chicago "pigs" last summer. Yet, ironically, these students (who were probably the first to give the Chicago "pigs" their name) called the professor the "pig."

Nothing was accomplished by beating up this professor. If anything, the students' cause was hurt. This violence shows that the SDS has gotten so wrapped up in the means toward its end that they have actually forgotten the end. And a low point in organized student radicalism has been hit—by the SDS.

If organized radicalism is to survive this low point, it must undergo a radical change. The organizations must employ more effective means toward radical goals. They must begin to use such arts as diplomacy. In other words, radical actions should be carried out to accomplish an end, not simply to break up furniture.

The high school underground in New York City received a rather impressive acknowledgment of their power from Norman Mailer during his campaign for the Democratic nomination for mayor. Mailer came to the high school commune to talk with the students who live there, as well as a student representing Stuyvesant High School's underground, Honest Bob Singer. In articles in both the *Herald Tribune* and the *Weakly Reader*, Honest Bob tells students why he thinks they should support Mailer.

MAILER AND BRESLIN
H. Bob Singer

It was about a week before the publication of this *Weakly Reader* that I went to a press conference for the high school underground for Norman Mailer (none of the candidates have talked even to official school papers). It was held in a commune that houses the H.S. Student Union and the H.S. Free Press, and most of the dramatis personae (in fact, everybody but me) were thereunto affiliated.

Mailer came in, shook hands all around, and made a phone call. Then he started talking about his 51st state plan. Everyone listened courteously, and no one asked if he and Breslin were "serious"—that question occurs only to people hypnotized by Big Politics—not these products (or rather the producers) of New Politics and New Media, it's not they who have to be told Mailer

WEAKLY
READER
No. 13
New York

is serious, dead (to be quite melodramatic) serious.

But while he talked, there seemed to be a wall coming up between him and my colleagues. Bad vibrations, you know. I couldn't figure out what it was—being as I am an old fellow of the Mailer-can-do-no-wrong school—until this girl there shook her head and told him point-blank that his program just isn't "revolutionary."

I couldn't see the point of this objection and neither, so the vibes indicated, could Mailer (which excuses *me*). He tried to explain the importance of meeting the needs of the people, of giving the people of the city what they basically, humanly, need in order to make existence bearable. She told him that to improve people's lots in the existing society wouldn't advance their revolutionary struggle. He explained that the people want and need to control their own destinies, to determine their own life-styles, to create decent, viable, inhabitable communities. She said that this wouldn't hurt capitalism.

Well, this girl wasn't all wrong. Giving 8 million people the power to determine their own political destiny may not shake American politics to its reactionary roots. Nixon may not worry if the inner-city dwellers can control their communities, clean up the slums, and get adequate food, medical services, etc. Imperialism won't crumble, probably, if a community in New York City can—and does—abolish capitalism in its own limits, and certainly racism won't end if people are free to determine their own life-styles. These peachy things won't follow, said the girl, and it seems sadly true.

But Mailer says they will. Why? Well, he says, for himself and Jimmy Breslin to get elected, a fantastic sleeping political giant will have to be awakened. People are sick of the city and often show it by shlumpfing for an endless procession of ward-heelers and hacks. If all this bottled disgust with urban living can be unstoppered by the hope it will take to get radically different (not to say revolutionary) candidates like Mailer and Breslin elected, it will stir up a political dynamo that will just not stop unsatisfied. Ultimately, the people will get what they want—or else something else will blow up. If the first, great. If the second, dynamite! And if that's not revolution, honey, what is?

Mailer and Breslin are running on a pre-ideological platform of human rights and dignity. Their merits have been recognized by the givers of America's highest literary awards and by the millions of readers of the old *Herald Tribune* and the *Post*. They know, understand, and love the city and its people and are completely at the disposal of the people and their needs. They both believe in Power to the People—a doctrine of the Left and Right, and denied only by the Idiot Middle. Help them get in—

Support Them! Vote for Them!

        Students are forming power organizations all over the country. They are trying to take the power that has been denied them.

Examples of this are given in *Iceberg!*, a high school underground paper that reaches high schools throughout the South.

WHAT'S HAPPENING . . .

OAK RIDGE, TENN.—About 150 people attended a meeting in Oak Ridge to discuss the problems in their school. Among the dissatisfied were about 25 concerned parents, and about 25 hecklers. A few of

ICEBERG
No. 1
Nashville,
Tennessee

the things discussed were repression of students by the administration, a critical analysis of the school curriculum, and organizing to combat school policies. By the end of the meeting, the would-be hecklers realized the sincerity of the others, and seemed willing to join in the struggle. During the meeting, many of the parents had valuable suggestions, and observed with curiosity. About 15 members of the group expressed interest in putting out a paper, and it will probably be out shortly.

NEW ORLEANS, LA.—Several New Orleans High Schools have formed a city-wide chapter of SDS. So far they have organized demonstrations to protest various aspects of school and community policy. The most successful were the protests against the American Legion, and a protest against the oppressive policies of the school system. The group, which has had to deal with many forms of repression, is now irregularly printing an underground rag, *The Finger*.

CHARLOTTE, N.C.—Several area high schools in Charlotte are now on the move. The *Inquisition* is a really together rag which some of the students are putting out. Should expect to be hearing from Charlotte more in the near future.

RICHMOND, VA.—A few months ago, a bunch of Richmond high school students formed the Hermitage Student Union, a group which had presented various demands to the administration. Among the demands was the formation of an Afro-American histories course, academic freedom, and revision of dress codes. The repression the group received was unbelievable. Several of the leaders were kicked out of school, kids were beaten up by their parents for participating, and the FBI cooperated with local authorities in harassing one guy. One student was shot, not badly, in the back by local right-wingers. More than anything, this group needs moral support.

LAKELAND, FLA.—Radical high school students from Lakeland, Florida, attended a student government meeting and demanded representation for their newly formed group, The Concerned Students Council. They got it and are now making radical demands of the SGA. It was discovered that the SGA planned to do "whatever necessary" to stop their group. The CSC is now part of a larger group, The Bay Area Coalition, which recently held a demonstration in Tallahassee of 500 students.

NASHVILLE, TENN.—About sixty high school students from Nashville have formed the Nashville Student Union. They have already held several conferences and had workshops on various interesting issues. In a recent meeting, they decided to constitute a draft counseling program, and set up a ring of students to learn how to counsel. They have been receiving support from sections of the adult community. And they plan to have more conferences in the future.

SWAN-QUARTER, N.C. (HIPS)—More than 800 black students have been boycotting classes to protest the Swan-Quarter County integration plan which would utilize only the white schools. The black students are fighting for a new plan under which white students would attend two black schools in addition to the present effort to desegregate the white schools. The county welfare department, in an attempt to smash the boycott, stopped all welfare payments going to those families that have children participating in the protests. On Nov. 12th, at a demonstration in the county courthouse to protest the welfare cut, police threw smoke bombs into the building and closed the courthouse doors to prevent any of the high school students from getting out. In desperation, a 17-year-old girl finally jumped out of a second story window. The police then opened the doors and arrested forty-seven of the high school students.

ATLANTA, GA.—Students from about four or five De Kalb and Fulton County high schools now have active student movements in progress. *The Grady Grope*, a high school underground newspaper, printed a poem written by a student from Columbia High School. The student was suspended, and a support demonstration drew about 100 students. A city-wide meeting of Atlanta high schoolers is scheduled for Saturday, Jan. 18th, and more conferences are expected in the future. Presently, Atlanta students are being kicked out of school for distributing *The Great Speckled Bird*, Atlanta's underground paper, and for long hair and dress.

High School Students Of the City, Unite!

THE AWAKENED COMMUNITY
WILL SEE ITS DEMANDS
REALIZED; THE STRIKE
WILL CONTINUE.

Since much of the writing about student power talks about the demands of black students (for example, Afro-American studies, more black teachers), you might think that the high school black power organizations work closely with the high school underground. In most cases, this isn't so. The "Spring

SIX   Black Power for the Black Students

Offensive" article in the *High School Free Press* spoke a lot about white students working together with blacks for the needs of blacks, but the spring offensive constituted the first time that black and white student organizations really worked together to pass the demands of a black student organization. For this reason, many New York high school radicals considered the spring offensive to be a milestone in unifying young radicals.

The New York Student Union had been really working at trying to get together with black high school student organizations, the Black Student Union and the Afro-American Students' Association. However, other high school underground organizations around the country have not considered this to be one of their main objectives. They have been very interested in meeting the needs of black students and representing their ideas in the underground papers, but, for the most part, the functions of the organizations have remained separate. One reason for this is the need that many students, especially black students, see for being separate and thus creating pride in the separate identity of the Afro-American.

In my school, for instance, there was not a satisfactory representation of Afro-American students on the *Smuff* staff. Yes, we had a black student on the staff and a black contributor, but we couldn't very honestly have put them in front of us and claimed this as adequate representation of a black student population that was more than 10 per cent of the school. And many of the rest of the black students in the school told us that they were not interested in joining *Smuff* because they saw it as a white organization. In Hackensack, we did have an Afro-American Society, a club with faculty sponsors, and some of their ideas were represented in *Smuff*. However, no white students were members of the Society and they were not welcome to join it. The Afro-American Society was not really a black power organization, although the members were interested in black power. The Society was a worthwhile club, but it did not really have any movement going for it. And toward the end of the year, the number of members who attended meetings was on a considerable decline.

Other black high school organizations around the country (not only in New York) are much more active. And where they are active, they get good coverage in the underground press.

The following article illustrates what is often the relationship between a black-power organization and a high school underground paper.

BLACK PEACESTONE RANGERS RAP TO MSA

THE OPEN DOOR
Vol. I, No. 3
Milwaukee,
Wisconsin

A few weeks ago Jim, Wes, and I (Mark) set up an interview with a group of black high school students. Their organization is named the Black Peacestone Rangers. It is a militant black nationalist group and we wanted to get their opinions of the schools and other ideas and present them to you, the readers. The interview was tape recorded and we talked a lot to the black students off the tape about *The Open Door* and *The Milwaukee Student Alliance* because the black students were somewhat suspicious of us and *The Open Door* and our purpose for an interview. The article is not really an interview but more like a discussion between us. We would be interested in your response to the article so please write us letters containing your ideas or your reaction to the black students' ideas.

Mark Butterworth

JIM: What are black students doing in the high schools right now? Are they getting organized?

BL. ST: The black students in the high schools are getting ready, but some of them feel that all of them are not ready to do anything. They just want to keep their cool until they are sure they can do something and pull it off without anyone getting picked off.

WES: What specifically do black students feel is wrong with the schools?

BL. ST: In the school I go to, and most other schools, the teachers aren't ready to teach us what we want to learn. A lot of us black students would like to have our own people teaching us because then we would know we're getting a good education. And when I say our own people, I don't mean Negroes either, I mean blacks.

BL. ST: The main thing is teaching black history, because to know one's history is to know oneself. How's a man going to appreciate his own people if he doesn't know anything about them? If you just exist, if you don't have any past, then you really can't appreciate yourself. I think that if they intermingle black history with regular U.S. history, they'll miss a lot and they won't put in as much as they would if there was a separate course for U.S. and black history.

JIM: I was wondering if you could give some examples of racism in Milwaukee public schools?

BL. ST: Yeh. I go to Custer, you know, and now take the basketball team for instance. Let's say you're a black student and you're a good player, but there's a white kid who's a good basketball player, but not just as good as you. He'll get the job. You have to be twice as good as the white athletes to make the team. Like you know Washington, Johnny Washington, he's an out of sight athlete, isn't he? And he's got to be twice as good as the white athlete before he could make the team.

BL. ST: The teachers, as far as grades are concerned— I mean you really don't have any concrete evidence against them—but if you are a black student—you can tell if you're getting the right grades you deserve and class is going the way it's supposed to—and many times the teacher shows discrimination in the classes.

BL. ST: They give us a third degree education so they can give us a diploma, but then you go to jobs and you don't know that much—you don't know as much as you should.

BL. ST: I know that down South, if you pick potatoes, they'll give you a diploma.

MARK: What do you want done in the high schools— not maybe just for the black students—but for all students?

BL. ST: Myself, I can't speak for all students because we black students have enough problems of our own. Now, we can only speak for ourselves. For one, the Milwaukee public school system and all systems don't concern black people at all. The system is set up for white people in a white society. So therefore black people won't get anything out of the system, or know anything but what the white man wants him to know, unless he gets together and starts his own black schools to learn about his own black things.

BL. ST: I want all the school conditions changed, you know, like the blackboards and windows that are broken out—they don't have much heat and all that—and they won't until they get the windows fixed.

BL. ST: What do you think should be done about the wrongs of the schools, Mark? We think the first thing is that the students have to stop thinking that someone has to tell them how to think and what to do and how to live their lives and that they have to be forced to do this and have to be forced to believe what someone tells them to believe, that this is the way the United States is and this is the way they have to live and they have to grow up and become part of the status quo which keeps not only black people down but all poor people. They have to start thinking about themselves and freedom for themselves.

BL. ST: Black people *are* thinking freedom for themselves but most of their thinking is not inside the school, most of their thinking is outside the school, but they are thinking about freedom for themselves.

BL. ST: What do you think should be done in the Milwaukee public schools?

WES: I think, more or less, that if you feel you can *learn* separately, it would be better. That's the way it ought to be because otherwise you're not learning—nobody's learning in the school system now—and you can't learn what you are.

BL. ST: We learn everything in the school system that we don't want to learn—we learn everything that's not relevant to us—that's what we learn.

BL. ST: But when I went to school—I don't go to school now—they were teaching white history. Don't you think you learn enough about white history?

JIM: No. We're learning very little about white history because we're learning a lot of lies. Like what I do —I don't even look at the history book. I've been doing a lot of outside reading and a lot of other things— looking at things, rapping to people, and things like that—and I've learned a lot of things I'd never learn in that history class, because they're afraid to teach it.

MARK: It's like he said. The black students are learning outside of schools; they're learning what they want to learn, what they think is relevant to themselves. We think that the education we're getting in schools is a bunch of junk; it's garbage. The education inside the public schools has to be made relevant, not only to the black students but all students.

BL. ST: If the white students in the Milwaukee public schools don't think the education is relevant, why don't they get together and do something about it?

JIM: They're starting to get together and do something about it.

BL. ST: Even though they're afraid of us learning about what's happening with the Panthers, whether they teach it to us or we teach it to ourselves, what's going to happen is going to happen anyway. Because whether they teach us the truth or we find out the truth ourselves, the truth is going to be found out.

JIM: See, that's what's wrong with this society. They can tell you what they want to tell you and what they want you to believe, but you can see around you that it's not true. They tell you that there's equality, but you can look around at the schools and you know there's not equality. And they just mess themselves up by telling you a lot of lies when everything around you contradicts them.

WES: What do you think about Vietnam?

BL. ST: The only problem we've got with Vietnam is how we're going to get all the black people out of there.

JIM: Yeh. The Vietnamese are fighting a similar struggle to yours. The United States is keeping the Vietnamese down the same way it's keeping the black people down.

WES: And the reason the Vietnamese are winning is because the people are all together.

BL. ST: You know, only 17 per cent of the world is white, but he's trying to claim the whole world. He went into Africa and everyplace else. But he knows he's getting kicked out of the rest of the places now, so he's trying to get into others, to control them so he can control the whole world. But the only thing he's going to do is start a war and lose because 17 per cent of the world's population can't control the rest.

JIM: But 17 per cent of the people don't really control the world—only a small minority of them do. Poor white people don't have control over their lives either. It's just like Milwaukee. A lot of white students have it very good, but South Division is one of the worst schools around and it's in a poor white neighborhood, a Spanish-speaking neighborhood. It's considered a ghetto school—it's one of the worst schools in the city of Milwaukee. They have the worst teachers, like black schools. It's almost the same. They're poor white and Spanish speaking. Pulaski is a little better, but it's not as good as some school in the suburbs because those people out there are richer and they get a better education. In white society there's discrimination too. White people are shitting on themselves, besides shitting on black people.

White students often talk about the problems of racism themselves when not enough black students are interested in expressing their point of view in a white newspaper. Racial problems constitute a popular theme for any media, and the underground press is far from an exception.

These articles bring up an interesting question for the high school underground. If the student is a nigger, what is the black student? Most writers conclude indirectly (even if they never thought of the question) that the black student is treated even more like a nigger than is the white student. The high schools have done an even poorer job of meeting the needs of the black students than they have of meeting the needs of the white students. (I agree, but I believe that the high school administrations are putting in a genuine effort to change this. Many schools, like mine, for instance, now are offering Afro-American Studies courses.)

Anyhow, here are some articles by white students about the black students.

A CASE OF THE STUDENT AS NIGGER AND RACIST

THE OPEN DOOR
Vol. I, No. 3
Milwaukee,
Wisconsin

Racism is a frightening thing, but it's even worse when you find it in your friends or classmates.

At my school, Nicolet, racism is becoming increasingly apparent. When in my world history class we got to discussing civil rights, I was appalled to hear someone start talking about how all blacks (he called them "those colored people") are inherently lazy, no good, and generally less intelligent than whites.

When a friend and I started trying to tell him about the basically racist atmosphere that blacks in this country are confronted with from birth, he was joined by three or four others who started yelling about white superiority and how no black has ever done anything worthwhile. They said all this with such great conviction it was frightening.

The majority of kids in that and other classes are abysmally uninformed. I have heard people confidently telling others that all blacks are parasites on white society, while Martin Luther King, Eldridge Cleaver, and innumerable others have done more to wake up the world to human injustice than anyone else. They believe that the American Indian is perfectly content and well off on his reservation, while he is in reality being starved by the government of land that is rightfully his, having his hunting and fishing rights taken from him, and having almost every treaty ever made with him broken. They have implict faith and trust in anything they are told by a hypocritical government or teacher, and accept without question that the United States is liberating the Vietnamese peasants and that the NLF will trample them out of existence if they win, when in reality it's the other way around.

This faith does not come out of stupidity, but is formed by twelve years of indoctrination in the schools where students are taught to respect and fear the authority of the establishment, represented by the teacher. By the time they graduate from high school, most students are so thoroughly brainwashed that they would never think of questioning anything they are told.

Until people are exposed to the truth and know what is really happening in this country, attitudes like these will flourish, creating a new generation of racist oppressors. It is an important responsibility of our school systems to furnish the opportunity for students to learn the truth, and stop the flow of propaganda and hypocrisy with which students are now being indoctrinated.

THOUGHTS ON A BAD SCENE
John Franklin

Hi, class! Let's get out our notebooks and turn to the cliche section. Everyone found it? Good. Okay, the two we'll be using today are "The Long Hot Summer" and "It Can't Happen Here."

IN-BETWEEN
Vol. I, No. 8
Hamilton, Ohio

You are undoubtedly familiar with them both. The first is rather recent—started in this place called Watts and did a road tour: Detroit, Newark, Cincinnati, and all over, scaring upright, honest, fine middle class citizens. Terrible. It also made things rough for a few innocent blacks but who cares? That'll teach 'em to live in places like that.

Nothing to get *too* scared of, though. We all know a little Mace and an enthusiastic riot squad is all it takes to cure it. Besides, there's always our second cliche, a real bit of folk wisdom. Remember when you had nightmares, and your mother would say, "Don't sweat the bogey man, honey, it can't happen here"?

I never was too good at listening to my mother, though. It *can* happen here, and it's going to, unless something is done and fast. This nightmare is for real, and it has been lurking outside for quite a while. Recent events have opened the door. I won't go into a history of the past two weeks. If you are interested you already know about them. A police officer did sum it up pretty well last Saturday night when he radioed, "What we've got here is an armed camp."

It won't do just to slam the door and ignore the situation again. The bogey man is inside now, and he's hungry. Long overdue changes will have to be made. We need a concerned and responsive city government, councilors who are aware of what's happening and who will take the needed action. The police department will have to be improved with new men and a new attitude. The whole community must wake up and dedicate itself to erasing racism and inequality, with the ultimate goal of a truly integrated city with the "South End" just an ugly memory.

There is hope; just since Tuesday, there have been marked changes, most noticeably in the attitudes of the city officials and in the editorial policy of the *Middletown Journal*. There is talk of black police officers, and a black reporter for the newspaper. A citizens' committee is being formed to work on the Community Center and other such matters.

It's a start, but there's still much to be done. Everyone should become involved. Put pressure on the local government and other authorities to let them know that action must be taken. Volunteer to help with the changes. Most important, work to end racist thinking throughout the city. The scars of a full-blown riot never heal. Is our continued apathy and complacency worth the price?

ANALYSIS: NEAT AND CLEAN WITH *JULIA*
F. B. J.

THE AMERICAN REVELATION
Vol. I, No. 6
Elgin, Illinois

It's too bad our society has to have a television show like *Julia*. But *Julia* is straight white society's way of showing straight black society that the Tee Vee industry is following the Kerner Commission's recommendations to place more blacks on the mass media. Since the beginning of the Tee Vee industry the inane, sentimental, weak-minded junk on the boob tube has been of, by, and for white people. Now with the advent of accelerated tokenism the black people have been dragged into the garbage on the twenty-inch screen.

What is so degrading about *Julia*? Well, in order to become palatable to the Tee Vee watchers and to prove the white liberal's hypothesis that anyone regardless of his skin color can become "white," Julia had to be a "Good One." Julia lives in a "clean place" (how nice), and has her son say his prayers *every night* (how Godly!), does not talk loudly or drink much (how de-

cent!). Best of all Julia's deceased husband was an officer (an officer, how wonderful!) killed in Vietnam (how
patriotically American!).

Oh, Purity, Wholesomeness, and Whiteness! This
show is not only the first series about a black family,
it is the first series about a saint. Yes, St. Julia has
really made it white.

Julia is typical of straight white society's reaction
to freedom riding and burning ghettos and it is indeed
sad to think that a black *Ozzie and Harriet* thing is all
that will replace *Amos and Andy* and that Diahann
(Saint) Carroll is all that will replace Hattie (Mammy)
McDaniel (regardless of the fact that Miss Carroll looks
so much finer). It is even sadder to think that many
black people will be satisfied by this cop-out tokenism.

Julia is not without redemptive qualities. Its photography is good, especially for television; and the absence
of that corny canned applause is a true blessing. But
the fact that it opts out to the racist middle class far
overshadows any technical quality.

A cynic may find it mildly amusing to think about
the results of straight white society trying to pacify that
other dissenting group in America, the white left, in
this same manner. Can you imagine watching *Ricky
the Resister* or *The Ben Spock Show* (live from the
federal pen)? But think for a moment. We already have
a little black girl getting crowned by Imperial Margarine
and a grown black woman expounding on the virtues
of Green Bleaching Crystals.

These thoughts are not quite so jolly when you watch
Julia. Further cop-outs must not be far off.

A PALEFACE ON *SOUL ON ICE*
F. B. J.

THE AMERICAN
REVELATION
Vol. I, No. 7
Elgin, Illinois

What is a brown-haired, blue-eyed honky like me doing reading *Soul on Ice* by Black Panther leader Eldridge Cleaver? Well, I'm doing what all whites, especially young whites, should be doing: getting into the ideas of a great revolutionary philosopher. There are three reasons why us ofays should check out Cleaver's literary masterpiece:

Literary Checkout Reason # 1: Relating

It's easy for even a KKK member to understand the motives of a "bootlicking Uncle Tom," so Toms are well accepted. But the establishment (white and black) hates and fears Eldridge Cleaver because he talks like a man true to himself. They can't understand a man like that, they haven't even read him. They must hear the real funk of the race struggle as Cleaver tells it, so here it is—white man's desire for sexual superiority. After relegating black men to the role of Supermasculine Menials in society, white men assumed the roles of Omnipotent Administrators. The Administrators assigned all physical tasks to the Menials, and took on all intellectual work themselves. However, since sexuality is physical, the Administrators (sensing a need for sex as a part of their lives) claimed sexual superiority over the Menials. Yet the Administrators could not help feeling sexually jealous of the Menials whom they had encouraged to become athletically and musically proficient. So the Administrators lynched, tarred and feathered, and castrated Menials in a perverted attempt to prove their sexual prowess.

In this same fantasy-reality vein, Cleaver explains

the positions of white women (the Superfeminines) and black women (the Amazons) in society and their attitudes toward their men, white men and black women having access to each other as well as mates of their own races, and black men and white women being forever separated.

Literary Checkout Reason #2: Speaking

Eldridge Cleaver speaks out against much of America's corrupt history and society: its heroes, puritanism, foreign policy, and prisons. He comments on Norman Mailer, the white author, and James Baldwin, the black author, and the irony of their cultural directions, Mailer toward Africa, Baldwin toward Europe.

Literary Checkout Reason #3: Writing

Cleaver is probably the most talented writer to arrive on the literary wasteland of this decade. He is a master of *living* language and writes in a poetic prose which fascinates anyone—*anyone*—who reads it.

Eldridge Cleaver is now an exile, driven out by the Honko-Cossaks who control this country, its courts, and its prisons. Those black and white radicals who remain should study *Soul on Ice* and carry on the ideas of its author, Eldridge Cleaver.

Black students also write about themselves . . .

ON THE BLACK MOVEMENT
Norma Williams

ENRAGÉ
Vol. I, No. 2
New York

The New Left today is generally defined as a coalition of the three oppressed groups in society: blacks, students, and workers. However, if we look closely at the accomplishments of the New Left over the past few years, we see that they were few and even if they did change some part of the society, it was a small part which left the basic structure unchanged (e.g. many people believe that one reason Johnson did not run again was due to the unrest in the country brought on by the Left. However, who was elected this past November? Nixon. The basic structure has not changed).

Why has this coalition all but failed heretofore? Before answering that question (if it can be answered), I will list four preconditions which are necessary for viable coalitions: (a) recognition by the parties involved of their respective self-interests; (b) the mutual belief that each party stands to benefit in terms of that self-interest from allying with the other or others; (c) the acceptance of the fact that each party has its own independent base of power and does not depend for ultimate decision-making on a force outside itself; and (d) the realization that the coalition deals with specific and identifiable goals as opposed to general and vague ones. Considering these four preconditions, I will show why "one-third" of this coalition has been unsuccessful: the relationship between blacks and white workers.

Even if one accepts that, in terms of oppression, blacks and white workers are equal, he will agree that, in terms of how they are regarded by society, they are not. That is, a black man and a white man can be in the same economic and social rut but the fact that the latter is white increases his chances of getting out of the rut. This is not true only in our age: In the early years of America when both whites and blacks were indentured servants, it was a great deal easier for a white servant to run away and merge into the general population than it was for a black one. Or later (beginning in Louisiana in 1898), "grandfather clauses" were passed—laws which granted the right to vote to all those whose grandfathers had voted. This enfranchised even the poor and illiterate whites who earlier had been in a political situation almost as bad as that which the blacks were in. A final example is that of the immigrants whose task of assimilation was a great deal easier not only because they arrived at a time when America needed the semi and unskilled labor but also because of their race. It is this "You're white, you're right. If you're black, stay back," attitude which has made the second precondition inoperable: in most cases, white workers feel that allying with blacks will not help them satisfy their self-interests. They don't want the alliance either, because due to the "Advantage" of race they can achieve otherwise or because alliance with blacks could impede their own development (though slow it may be).

Most important of these preconditions (and one which unfortunately has succeeded least) is the third: the organization of independent power bases which have decision-making power. It is impossible to form any meaningful coalition unless each party has a power base to operate from and the other party (parties) recognizes it. It would be self-defeating for a stronger group to coalesce with a weaker one and, by the same token, in the end it would be suicidal for a weaker group to coalesce with a stronger one. The blacks (for I believe that, at present, the blacks, to obtain the necessary power base, will have to work harder than the white workers) must not concentrate major efforts in coalescing with ANY other group: First there must be organization WITHIN—then the coalition. Otherwise, as has already been illustrated, the coalition will be a powerless, disorganized, and insecure one. I personally do not fear that when and if all parties are strong, they will not need each other. No matter how strong either the blacks or the workers or the students may become individually, neither alone will be strong enough to alter the basic structure of the government.

In regard to this power base a final point can be made: It is needed for security, the security of the group which is to enter the coalition. No group should be so dependent on another group, which by definition (precondition *a*) has its own respective self-interests. True, it is expected that the interests of one group will coincide with those of the other group(s), but what if they don't? What if the workers desire a change but the blacks do not and the blacks are the stronger of the two? Then the workers are left helpless. In this particular relation (i.e. between blacks and workers) this is especially liable to happen due to economic competition (a result of self-interest) which could take place. This too has happened previously in history, two examples being the Populist Movement in the 1880's and the 1890's and the role of whites in different originally black organizations. When the white support dies, so does the movement. The lesson to be learned from this is that unless each party within a coalition has a power base, and this power base is recognized by the other party (parties), the weaker party is going to be a scapegoat and will not truly gain anything.

The final precondition—the realization that the coalition deals with specific and identifiable as opposed to general and vague goals—is also important.

So—back to the original question: Why has this coalition (now meaning blacks, workers, and students) all but failed heretofore? In my opinion, it is due to the fact that these four preconditions have not been applied. There are other possible reasons, of course (e.g. many of the members of these three groups do not believe that they are truly oppressed or that those who do possess power have kept the powerless in such bitter antagonism against each other that they haven't been able to see who the real enemy is), but through a massive re-education program, these stumbling blocks can be eliminated. The coalition is needed and it should operate as do different groups in a war: One group may be in the air dropping bombs. Another might be on the ground in direct combat. Another might be in an office planning strategy, and so on. They are all "taking care of business" and if they are doing so successfully, each knows what the other is doing. True, they are all performing different tasks but their ultimate goal is the same: TO WIN!!!!!!!

Sources: Stokely Carmichael and Charles Hamilton, *Black Power—the Politics of Liberation in America*; Benjamin Quarles, *The Negro in the Making of America*.

But again, the New York high school students seem to have the most unity between black and white radical movements. The following articles represent a milestone, when black and Puerto Rican students' demands were presented in the *New York High School Free Press*. After that, "freeing the Panther 21" became a major issue for the Student Union, as well as for the black student organizations.

Personally, I would prefer to see racial groups come together in a more peaceful way, but there is a value in it happening this way. I am very optimistic about the racial situation with my generation. Of course, bigotry and hatred are still strong, but they are dying. I look forward to a time when there will be no more need for black-power organizations or student-power organizations, for that matter.

NOW!

BLACK AND PUERTO RICAN CITYWIDE HIGH SCHOOL COUNCIL
DEMAND:

1—No more automatic suspensions of H.S. students. *2*—No more police and police aides inside NYC high schools. *3*—Strict adherence to fire regulations—doors to schools must be left open. *4*—Open the school daily to parent observation. *5*—Community rehabilitation centers should be allowed to set up programs to treat known drug addicts. *6*—Elimination of the general course of study. *7*—Because of the total chaos in education this year, the suspension of all Regents exams this June. *8*—Recognition by all NYC schools of the two Black holidays, May 19th—Malcolm X's Birthday, and January 15th—Dr. King's birthday. *9*—Immediate alteration of teaching population and examination to supply Black educators proportionate to the student population. *10*—Complete examination of all books and educational supplies used by the schools. *11*—The creation of school clubs along ethnic lines with facilities and funds from the school G.O. *12*—improved conditions for the students in school such as music in the lunchroom, more dances, improved athletic programs with rifle clubs and self-defense classes. *13*—Teachers who are teaching a course should have a background related to the course. *14*—Creation of Student-Faculty (equal representation) Council in each school which will make binding decisions on the following matters: curriculum, school staff, discipline, rules and regulations, etc. *15*—The reorganization of high schools by September 1969, along community lines, so that black students will not be forced to go to hostile communities to seek an education.

THE NEW YORK HIGH SCHOOL STUDENT UNION DEMANDS:

1—No suspensions, involuntary transfers, exclusion from classes, detention, harassment of students. Due process for students. 2—No cops in schools, no narcos, security guards, plain clothesmen, informers. 3—No program cards, hall checks, ID's, passes. 4—An end to commercial and general diplomas, one diploma for every student upon graduation. 5—Open admissions to colleges, a college education free for everyone who wants one. 6—Jobs and housing for every student who wants them on graduating, dropping out, or leaving home. The army is not a decent job. 7—No military recruiting in schools, no military assemblies, literature, no sending names to draft boards or recruiters. An immediate end to the draft. 8—Black and Latin departments controlled by Black and Latin students. 9—Community control of the schools, and every other community facility. Students are part of the community. 10—POWER! Student control of curriculum, publications, assemblies, clubs, student government, dress, etc. The right to organize politically. 11—We support the fifteen points of the Black and Puerto Rican Citywide HS Council.

THE TEN-POINT PROGRAM AND PLATFORM FOR BLACK STUDENT UNIONS

We want an education for our people that exposes the true nature of this decadent American society. We want an education that teaches us our true history and role in the present-day society.

We believe in an educational system that will give our people a knowledge of self. If a man does not have knowledge of himself and his position in society and the world then he has little chance to relate to anything else.

1. WE WANT FREEDOM; WE WANT POWER TO DETERMINE THE DESTINY OF OUR SCHOOL.

We believe that we will not be free within the schools

to get a decent education unless we are able to have a say and determine the destiny of our people.

2. WE WANT FULL ENROLLMENT IN THE SCHOOLS FOR OUR PEOPLE.

We believe that the city and federal government is responsible and obligated to give every man a decent education.

3. WE WANT AN END TO THE ROBBERY BY THE WHITE MAN OF OUR BLACK COMMUNITY.

We believe that this racist government has robbed us of an education. We believe that this racist capitalist government has robbed the Black Community of its money by forcing us to pay higher taxes for less quality.

4. WE WANT DECENT EDUCATIONAL FACILITIES, FOR THE USE OF STUDENTS.

We believe that if these businessmen will not give decent facilities to our community schools, then the schools and their facilities should be taken out of the hands of these few individual racists and placed into the hands of the community, with government aid, so the community can develop a decent and suitable educational system.

5. WE WANT AN EDUCATION FOR OUR PEOPLE THAT TEACHES US HOW TO SURVIVE IN THE PRESENT DAY SOCIETY.

We believe that if the educational system does not teach us how to survive in society and the world, it loses its meaning for existence.

6. WE WANT ALL RACIST TEACHERS TO BE EXCLUDED AND RESTRICTED FROM ALL PUBLIC SCHOOLS.

We believe that if the teacher in a school is acting in a racist fashion, then that teacher is not interested in the welfare or development of the students, but only in their destruction.

7. WE WANT AN IMMEDIATE END TO POLICE BRUTALITY AND MURDER OF BLACK PEOPLE. WE WANT ALL POLICE AND SPECIAL AGENTS TO BE EXCLUDED AND RESTRICTED FROM SCHOOL PREMISES.

We believe that there should be an end to harassment by the police department of Black people. We believe that if all of the police were pulled out of the schools, the schools would become more functional.

8. WE WANT ALL STUDENTS THAT HAVE BEEN EXEMPT, EXPELLED, OR SUSPENDED FROM SCHOOL TO BE REINSTATED.

We believe all students should be reinstated because they haven't received fair and impartial judgment or have been put out because of incidents or situations that have occurred outside of the school's authority.

9. WE WANT ALL STUDENTS WHEN BROUGHT TO TRIAL TO BE TRIED IN A STUDENT COURT BY A JURY OF THEIR PEER GROUP OR STUDENTS OF THEIR SCHOOL.

We believe that the student courts should follow the United States Constitution so that students can receive a fair trial. The Fourteenth Amendment of the U.S. Constitution gives a man a right to be tried by a jury of his peer group. A peer is a person from a similar economic, social, religious, geographical, environmental, historical, and racial background. To do this the court would be forced to select a jury of students from the community from which the defendents came. We have been and are being tried by a white principal, vice-principal, and white students that have no understanding of the "average reasoning man" of the Black Community.

10. WE WANT POWER, ENROLLMENT, EQUIPMENT, EDUCATION, TEACHERS, JUSTICE, AND PEACE.

As our major political objective, an assembly for the student body, in which only the students will be allowed to participate, for the purpose of determining the will of the students as to the school's destiny.

We hold these truths as being self-evident, that all men are created equal, that they are endowed by their creator with certain inalienable rights, that among these are life, liberty, and the pursuit of happiness. To secure these rights within the schools, governments are instituted among the students, deriving their just powers from the consent of the governed, that whenever any form of student government becomes destructive to these ends, it is the right of the students to alter or abolish it and to institute a new government, laying its foundation on such principles and organizing its power in such form as to them shall seem most likely to effect their safety and happiness. Prudence indeed will dictate that governments long established should not be changed for light and transient causes, and accordingly, all experiences have shown that mankind are more liable to suffer, while evils are sufferable, than to right themselves by abolishing the forms to which they are accustomed. But when a long train of abuses and force, pursuing invariably the same object, reveals a design to reduce them to absolute destruction, it is their right, it is their duty, to throw off such a government and to provide new guards for their future security.

HUNTER DEMANDS AND HSSU AND MORE

We, the Black and Puerto Rican students of Hunter College High School, feel that there are certain changes which must be made within Hunter that are long overdue and absolutely necessary if we are to become involved in a meaningful education. Hunter being a cross-section of the most brilliant girls in New York City, supposedly has the best education in this city, however, in many ways, the nature of the curriculum that is offered to students in this school reflects the attitudes that are so prevalent in this racist society in which we all live.

NEW YORK HERALD TRIBUNE No. 5 *New York*

We, as Black and Puerto Rican students, are particularly affected by this, as are Mexican-Americans, Indians, and other non-white students. There are too many aspects of the histories of these peoples that have been ignored or distorted; there are too many untruths and half-truths that students have been led to believe. Considering the nature of the conflicts that we are all involved in today, it does not seem unreasonable to demand that the roles of these peoples in history, past and present, be recognized as significant forces throughout all history and therefore should be dealt with as such. The students must play an important role in making these changes.

Foreign Languages: 1. Accept American Spanish as a different and not incorrect form. Puerto Rican and other American forms of Spanish are just as valid and decidedly more useful on this continent than Castilian Spanish. 2. Start an elective course in Kiswahili. We have chosen Swahili over 800 other African languages because it is the most widespread and is not connected with any one tribe. It is third among the most widely spoken African languages. It is probably one of the easiest African languages to learn since it is non-tonal and uses Roman script. Not only that, Swahili has a wealth of literature (particularly poetry) and has been a literary language centuries before the coming of the first Europeans in the sixteenth century.

Social Studies: 1. Start a compulsory course in the history of the Afro-American and Latin-American people in the U.S., to be taught by a qualified teacher, preferably one Latin-American and one Black. 2. Start a one year course that will deal with the effects of colonization on twentieth century Third World nations and their relationship today to Western "civilization." 3. Start a one year course that will deal with the effects of colonization of the Third World (Africa, Asia, Latin America), to be taught by a qualified teacher. 4. Recognize the African roots of certain aspects of Western civilization, and incorporate them into the already existing syllabus.

Faculty: In order to implement the above we feel that it is extremely necessary that all teachers be required to take a course that will enlighten them as to the history and culture of the various non-white groups and the present day implications that this has. A conscientious effort should be made to hire more Black, Puerto Rican, and Oriental teachers in order to reflect the racial composition of NYC.

Student Body: 1. A conscientious effort should be made to admit more Black, Puerto Rican, and Oriental students in order to reflect the racial composition of NYC. 2. A committee composed of students and faculty should be established for the purpose of evaluating the present entrance requirements and instituting a better system.

We would like to emphasize, once again, that we are demanding a meaningful role in instituting the above changes.

THE HIGH SCHOOL COALITION

"WE MUST RE-EDUCATE" is the adopted creed of the New York City Black High School Coalition. In our attempts to follow this creed to the letter, we have combined our efforts with several New York student groups to bring about total realization in all students of the detrimental nature of this decadent society. We have totally committed ourselves and our lives to the accomplishment of the goals we have set, the most important and basic being the "re-education" of the student, and Black students in particular. To this end, we, THE NEW YORK CITY BLACK HIGH SCHOOL COALITION, are dedicated.

THE NEW YORK CITY BLACK HIGH SCHOOL COALITION as a Black student group has been functioning on several

NEW YORK
HIGH SCHOOL
FREE PRESS
No. 8
New York

levels since April, 1968. At that time, Black student representatives from several Black high school student groups met in a series of grass roots conferences to discuss, analyze, and determine the fate of the Black student in New York City's high schools. At this time, it was realized by all present that the racist Board of Education, United Federation of Teachers, and various other forces of the system took special stock in the fact that the education the Black student up until then had been receiving served to keep him down in the future. In effect, it SERVED TO KEEP THE BLACK MAN "IN HIS PLACE." [A line is omitted in the article.] . . . izing this, and among the black people (with the exception of a few cases of "token" education) the Black students saw that a United Black Student Front was necessary in New York to achieve the overcoming of the system's forces. Later, after having gone back to their respective groups with the proposal for a United Black Student Front, it was resolved by the delegates that it was indeed necessary for them to form a Black student coalition.

The original groups represented at the United Black Student Front conferences were: THE N.Y.C. BLACK YOUTH ALLIANCE, THE UNITED FEDERATION OF HARLEM YOUTH, THE BLACK YOUTH FEDERATION, and THE AFRI-CAN-AMERICAN CULTURAL NATURALISTS FOR COMMUNITY UNITY AND ACTION. The Black Youth Alliance functioned in and around the St. Nicholas projects in Harlem, right off 125th Street, where many Black students from Brandeis, Haaren, Benjamin Franklin, Charles Evans Hughes, and other high schools in the Bronx and Brooklyn as well as Manhattan reside. The United Federation of Harlem Youth was composed of Black students in and out of high school living in the area of the Foster projects in Harlem, off 115th Street.

The Black Youth Federation comprised Black and Latin students from C. E. Hughes High School living in various sections of the Bronx, Brooklyn, Manhattan, and Queens. And finally, The African-American Cultural Naturalists was a Black organization of students from various Bronx schools.

The representatives of these four organizations were soon joined by representatives from several more, when on July 10th, several more Black student groups were allowed into the COALITION. The speed with which the COALITION spread, and the enthusiasm with which it was accepted, were important in making it the largest Black student organization in the city.

After having structured a program (the COALITION 11 POINT PROGRAM), and a constitution-manifesto, the New York City Black High School Coalition was moving!

In the month of June, 1968, the HIGH SCHOOL COALITION was less than two months old, and yet it was already suffering from the harassment given to opponents of the system. Two brothers, Brother Arthur Owens and Brother Wilbur Colom (interviewed in HSFP No. 1), had been harassed and beaten by the pigs outside of Brandeis and Haaren high schools after a program at which they tried to get Brother H. Rap Brown into the schools had been turned into a riot by the pig instigators. These two brothers, who had been the principal organizers of the first meetings of the HIGH SCHOOL COALITION, were then brutally beaten and then suspended from their schools.

Not deterred from their goals of re-education of the Black student, the N.Y.C. BLACK HIGH SCHOOL COALITION went on to struggle in a number of schools, gaining support as the battle flared. And then, it was June 30th and the systems forces just knew that everything was over. On June 30th, however, leaflets appeared throughout the school systems advising, "WE MUST ORGANIZE THIS SUMMER TO MEET THE CHALLENGES OF THE FALL!" The leaflets were distributed by the High School Coalition in an effort to awaken the Black student to the fact that June 30th represented a ceasefire to reorganize and rearm! One of the many ways the Black High

School Coalition rearmed the students was through the establishment of LIBERATION CLASSES. These classes were held daily, throughout the summer, and were taught by the students themselves, as well as by professional Black educators. The goals of classes were to make the student even more aware of the strained conditions surrounding him, and of their final total effect on his political conscience. The classes dealt with basically everything. There were classes in first aid; with actual practice. There were classes in photography, realizing the need of good photographers in a demonstration. There were classes in self-defense; arms theory; Maoism; Franz Fanon; Malcolm X and his basic philosophy; the Religions of Man, including Zen Buddhism, Islam, and Yoruba; Women in the Liberation Struggle; and films pertinent to each of these topics, as well as recordings and various other visual aids. Realizing that classes were not enough to re-educate the black student, the COALITION set about calling a series of rallies. The COALITION began to confirm their struggle and realize more fully the obstacles which had to be faced. Then came September, and with the coming of September, the annual teachers' strike.

This time, instead of admitting that money was still the basic issue, racist, capitalist, anti-semitic chairman of the UFT, Albert Shanker, painted a picture of job security and due process over the old worn out picture, thus presenting a new image for the teachers to fight behind, an image which led to the three month teachers' strike. And with the coming of the strike, the coming of a new battle for the BLACK HIGH SCHOOL COALITION. To enumerate on the number of conflicts the COALITION had with the pigs and the teachers during the strike would be useless. But just to give an idea, the opening of TAFT, BRANDEIS, HAAREN, SCIENCE and many other high schools was accomplished. In fact, before the strike was over, nearly every high school had been opened.

After the strike by the teachers, there were the week-long talks with the vice president of the Board of Education—no results. The High School Coalition had to find a new course for re-education of the Black student. They turned toward aiding the setting up of Afro-American Societies in every high school. On January 10th, 1969, a total of the results of their labors was taken. On that day, a CITY-WIDE AFRO-AMERICAN SOCIETY FORUM was called and officers of every Afro-American club were invited. The results were beautiful. Thirty schools in New York City had just gotten together in an effort to unite the bonds between the COALITION MEMBER ORGANIZATIONS. (An article on the forum will appear at a later date.) One of the goals of the forum was to accomplish a program for a Black student holiday. The day chosen was February 21st, Malcolm X's death day. Work was begun and the program was held on a city-wide level with two programs being held in each borough, and the best possible speakers being at each. This is the NEW YORK CITY BLACK HIGH SCHOOL COALITION, an organization based on the philosophy that students in this racist educational system must be re-educated. And we have set out to accomplish this re-education by any means necessary.

FREE THE PANTHER 21!!
Miriam Bokser

Long Island City High School. A strike and demonstration in support of Lonnie Epps, one of the Panther 21, who had been organizing a Black Student Union at the school. A rainy morning. Epps is still in jail. It's 8 a.m. and across from the school, down

NEW YORK
HIGH SCHOOL
FREE PRESS
No. 8
New York

the block, are a group of students, listening to some raps. The crowd seems to be mostly girls and is pretty evenly divided between black and white, including a few Puerto Rican kids.

The white kids aren't the upper bourgeois liberal types you see at demonstrations; their parents are probably prone to yelling "take a bath" or "if you don't like it here, why don't you go to Russia?" at anti-war and anti-draft demonstrations. The black kids don't all have naturals or leathers. Most of the black girls have straightened hair.

The raps. A black guy talks about the Panthers and Lonnie Epps for a few minutes. Someone else continues with the conditions of the school and the schools in general. Half the people pay attention. There is a lot of giggling. A young black guy starts to lead the group in some Panther chants, asking the guys and the girls to alternate phrases.

"No more pigs in our community."

"OFF THE PIG."

More giggling, etc., etc.

The strike seems disorganized. On the peripheries of the crowd, there are a lot of kids milling around; across the street is a luncheonette, and from there, watching the action, are about twenty black guys.

There are some cops along the next block which faces the school. They seem relaxed, having nothing to do.

Someone suggests a march around the school. A group of about fifty walk around the block, keeping to the sidewalks. There is more milling around and talking. The dean comes out and tries to convince the kids to come in. Some High School Union people talk to him and his logic falls apart; the students all seem to know where it's at. A group of black kids rapping. "You call yourself a Negro. Why don't you join us, man. You take Spanish 1; you know Negro means black." Some black guys are reading the Panther paper. And two black plainclothesmen leave the luncheonette and filter closer toward the crowd. People are hip to them and they finally leave.

The sophomores are arriving for school. It is 10:45. More kids join the group. At the corner near the school kids line up on either side of the street and begin to block it. The cops move over and try to clear the area. The kids begin to walk back and forth across the street, slowing down traffic. The cops keep trying to keep people on the sidewalks, but the people are having too much fun. The scene begins to get angry, but not uptight.

Gradually a decision is made to march. This time a group of about 200 start around the block. No one keeps to the sidewalks this time, although one of the more uptight "leaders" yells from time to time, "on the sidewalks!" The crowd surges into the streets, energy growing stronger and more definitely anti-pig.

As the people reach the block the front of the school faces, they find the cops lined up to prevent them from turning the corner. A few confrontations. A black girl goes up to the line and starts to walk through. Two pigs grab her arms and tell her to go back. She says, "Don't tell me where to go!" but they keep her back. She hassles them some more and then joins the group which by now is running down the next street. Past the First National City Bank, with due acknowledgment, and then return from the other side to the street facing the school. On this side there are no pigs. The strategy is to get more kids to join and continue walking, but people are fed up with walking so some folk start rapping again. The crowd splits into small groups.

A pig is hassling a black chick to get off a car she is sitting on. She says, "It must be your car for you to get so uptight!" He says, "Damn RIGHT!!" He begins to shove her and she says, "You don't have to push me. You're not my father or mother." He says, "Damn right, I'm not your father or mother." This remark falls like lead and she stands there glaring at him. He's so uptight and kind of confused and glares back at her. Her white friend who has been with her all morning glares at the pig too. He can't take the hostility and leaves. Some of the people decide to go to a showing of some Newsreel films in Flushing, a twenty minute ride on the subway. The group tries to interest others, and finally about thirty kids get on the train, and a lone cop guarding the Exit–No Entrance door doesn't hassle anyone for a school pass or money. The subway car loses a few of its more insidious ads.

The films. About thirty people crammed into a little room watching the Panther film. The screen is close-up. After the film there is a short discussion. Some of the kids talk about what they can do to keep the school uptight, the strike going. How to get the demands satisfied. They talk about the rotten principal and the difficulty in finding a meeting place. They mention that the Afro-American students club has an advisor who is always approving or disapproving the speakers and program. They talk about Lonnie Epps and how he may have been ahead of what the school was prepared for. A black guy mentions that mostly sisters were at the demonstration, that the brothers stayed across the street watching. That the brothers have got to start sharing the struggle with the sisters. There is more talk about organizing. About the fact that only three kids stayed out during the forty-five-minute strike at the end of November. The general feeling is that this is a good start, that finally the school is off its ass.

We see two more short films. The people dig them too and rap more about what they can do. They dig the fact that going off and getting stoned is no solution to their problems nor is setting themselves up in a confrontation with the pigs and getting massacred because of no preparation. They talk about organizing a group to go the next day to the Panther demonstration at

Center Street; a few elect themselves to write a leaflet.

So the first real action at Long Island City High School left everyone with a sense that something had actually been started, yet with a sense of reality about the lack of strength and the need to organize.

A common criticism of student radicals, in general, is that they put down everything and then offer no alternative. To an extent, this is a valid criticism. It is a lot easier to be destructive than creative. And, like other human beings, students often take the easiest way out. But this criticism is not entirely valid.

SEVEN   Educational Reform

A lot of adults close their ears after hearing only half of the students' story. This is understandable. They, too, are taking an easy way out.

Students in the underground offer no alternative, sometimes because there is no alternative. At least, there's no alternative that sounds like an alternative. With many restrictions, dress codes, for instance, the only alternative that the students want is no more dress codes.

Other times, concrete alternatives are being offered but not being taken seriously enough by the administration. Some of the alternatives have already been discussed in earlier chapters of this book. Meaningful student councils, self-censored and uncensored student newspapers, black studies courses, student power in general, these are all alternatives.

In fact, the underground itself is an alternative, and about as concrete an alternative as you will find. The underground press and the student-power organizations offer alternatives to students who are disillusioned with the overground counterparts.

This year, at my school, *Smuff* is offering another alternative, an independent study course that is run entirely by students. Our school has made ventures into the field of independent study for advanced students, but the subject matter and the independence of the student are restricted. Students have asked for independent study. Last year, the *Voice* had two editorials submitted that asked for it, and one of them was printed. But progress has not been made. "It takes time" is the excuse of most administrators. And perhaps for them it does. So now, the students who are involved with *Smuff* are doing it quickly.

The article that follows tells some more about the course and gives some students' opinions concerning the need for independent study.

THE STUDENT INDEPENDENT STUDY PROGRAM
Stephen Nyman

SMUFF
*Vol. II, No. 1
Hackensack,
New Jersey*

Everything that *Smuff* does is for one purpose only—to offer an alternative. We saw that things which should have been allowed to be said were smothered by the administration, so we said them. We say that Students are powerless, that they are "niggers," who can be abused and pushed around with no one to protest, especially the Students themselves. We see that Student freedoms can be "granted" and taken away as if they weren't basic rights, so we said that only the Students can get the power they must have to control their existences and we attempted to create a *Student Coalition* as an alternative to the mockery of "democratic power" embodied in the student council. And above all, we see that what is palmed off as an education is largely a collection of fact and information, a collection of required readings and required subjects and electives that have no meaning to our lives. Physics,

French, U.S. history, English all being taught (with the emphasis on the teaching not the learning) to get people into college, to complete requirements, to proliferate lies; being taught because they "have" to be taught, and being taught not to help us cope with and try to save the dying world we will take over or to help us cope with and save each other, but because they are on a list of "available subjects." The rationale of schools being a place where facts are transferred can no longer be accepted in a world where facts multiply every few years and additional fact-transferring courses will no more remedy the sickness than Afro-American studies will somehow inspire black awareness. The approach is only a century outmoded, and the school systems, run as they are by businessmen seeking a human output and kept stagnant by the influence of endless "community groups" and, I'm sorry to say, the all too large number of teachers tied to the past, aren't likely to wake up until it is too late, unless they can be coaxed and pinched *by the Students*. To offer a clear alternative *Smuff* will begin an *independent study program* run by and for the Students. To convince the administration that independent study programs must become an integral part of every school, not to please the pressure groups or anyone else, but for the sole benefit of the Students.

The history of independent studies supports their effectiveness even where they were created spontaneously. On the campuses of many colleges and universities where the Students went on strike, independent study groups were formed in apartments and dormitories to channel their thoughts into areas about which they wanted to learn and discuss at that moment in their lives, i.e., the direction of the movement, revolution, protest, the pros and cons of violence, etc. What they learned meant more to them than anything they were supposed to learn in the courses they would normally have attended. In Philadelphia there is a full-fledged program of independent studies—a school without walls—which has been a great success. There the Students learn U.S. history in the ghetto where history manifested itself, biology in the concrete jungle, on the banks of the polluted rivers where man has destroyed the biological balances, English from people who've lived. No one forced a course on them and no one deprived them of courses they wanted, because somebody out there understood that no one learns something he has no interest in. And if you say that Students won't learn something when they're out of the cage, it becomes obvious you were wasting your time with him in it. Scientists found out long ago that training (teaching) a porpoise to do tricks by holding out a fish (marks) simply made him into a reflection of his trainer (teacher) once he knew what he had to do to please his trainer . . .

It is quite clear that independent studies are a vital necessity and we know that they have worked elsewhere. Making them work here requires an evolution unique to this school and its Students. You, the reader, must take yourself seriously, taking your power as a Student seriously to create a program suited to you. *Smuff* will do all it can to organize the program and offer our own ideas and efforts, but revolution can only come from the people and the people are the Students.

Ideas, Plans, Thoughts and Organization—al clap (—trap)

Independent studies can go in two directions: they can be individuals learning on their own, or they can be study groups who communicate as Students and learn together. The former plan would no doubt be most appealing to the administrators since it varies little from making term papers or reports or standard crap and since it wouldn't involve Students gettin' together. No one will dispute that if the incentive were there or could be provided, the Student would learn quite a lot, pertinent to himself, but the communicative aspect is totally lost; there is no group experience and the Student remains firmly entrenched in his free-slave status. Individual studies would only continue a situation which does what Southern laws did to keep the "Niggero" in his place. He was kept from talking to all but a few other blacks and gathering in a group was strictly prohibited. Likewise, although there are several thousand Students in this school they can communicate with each other only very rarely, when they are not being told to shaddap while the teacher's talking. Student to Student communication is "too valuable" to "bother" to talk about Student power and there are no forums where a Student can speak and be spoken to by substantial numbers of Students. The Student population, fragmented by classes and courses, cannot realize its power nor the wealth of knowledge, opinions and life that is available among Students. *Smuff* must reject individual studies and support the study group plan to derive the most important benefits the program has to offer.

We plan to organize two experimental groups which would try out various approaches to learning and if they succeeded (in the opinion of the members) we could launch a much larger program. The first groups would have to choose between methods and invent new ones of their own.

"Supplementary studies," being anything that the group felt was not being given in their regular courses and which they wanted, could be not only productive but thoroughly revealing of the system's inadequacies. If a group member saw that a teacher (or many teachers, not necessarily his own) was passing over various points or was presenting badly slanted opinions or outright lies in the midst of facts ("most of what you hear is lies"), the group would research and discuss the subject to *find the truth*. The group could then publish a paper so that the Students (especially the Students in the classes that were not getting the truth) would have available to them an objective (or clearly opinionated) and well researched challenge to what the teacher(s) said was truth. On an even broader scale if an entire area of discussion was ignored by a teacher(s) the group could pursue it. (This would be where an in-depth study of revolution, our economic system, imperialism, ecological genocide or suicide, fascism in America, Mao, Lenin, Hitler, cbw, television as a subversive or protest-stimulating medium, freedom, or, as I think this list of subjects makes clear, anything anybody's on, would be useful.) Depending on the ambition of the group, they could as a group compile what they learned and thought into a book or a long paper and publish it for the Students on a school-wide basis. Supplementary studies would fill in the gaps, straighten out the twisted "facts," open new areas of thought to the Student and subject his own closely guarded opinions (too often not asked for by the teachers as if the teacher's opinion had more validity than the Student's) to the test of his own re-examination and scrutiny in the face of new philosophies and new worlds.

The debate (an informal, un-ruled debate) is sadly ignored by many teachers even though it is undisputably the easiest to arrange and most productive of all variations on the teaching method. Everyone has opinions and no one's opinions are so sacred and perfect that they can't be argued and possibly altered (I wonder how certain teachers would fare in a debate where they couldn't "give notes" and had to support their filthy prejudices). Debates are spontaneously generated animals and in the study group would be unrestricted by a middle-man teacher or his eternal preoccupation in getting all the "required work" finished. (I have a lustful desire to debate the high and mighty critics of *Smuff*, revolution, total freedom, student power, peace and an endless list of things dear to my heart. But they are probably not even perverting their lily-pure minds reading this . . . alas! . . . I wonder if they can be lured

198   OUR TIME IS NOW

out of their shells of self-proclaimed superiority over us lowly revolutionaries and back up their smug jibes in the open arena of a group . . .) I must stress the importance of the debate: If there is someone who believes things that you so totally oppose that you dismiss the person as an ass or a Neanderthal and consider it below your "dignity" to debate him you may find out that there are plenty of his kind around thinking the same way and all of them waiting for someone who speaks their language to come along. Calling a Marchi, a Wallace, a Yordi, a Proc, or a Hitler a pig and turning your head won't make them or their hidden legions go away or drive the hate from their hearts; but if you put him on the spot and make him tell you how by chanting "law and order" he can get it, he might fade away.

Along similar lines the group could try to solve problems, questions that many students are asking and others that they should be asking, as well as trying to come to some conclusions in respect to statements, assumptions and opinions we hear every day. Teachers, on occasion, try this sort of thing in their classes but they spend only one or two days, the classes are too large, the subject matter is restrained so that only on days when the teacher doesn't want to stick to his programmed program can anything of relevance be discussed, and the teacher will probably throw in his own personal "conclusion" to "wrap it up" anyway. The sort of problems would depend on the group, but for the first group one question could be whether a study program could be integrated into the regular system and whether a voluntary program like this could be largely substituted in place of the teaching system. Since I'm getting sick of hearing Walter Cronkite types say, "These young kids are out to tear down our glorious system without knowing what to put up instead of it, duhhh," why couldn't a study group get some idea of what the post-revolutionary world should be (whether you subscribe to the inevitability of the revolution or not). And those who shudder at the prospect of revolution could put revolutionaries and non-revolutionaries to work in deciding whether there is really any other way to change things. How 'bout "A society must have law and order to survive," "No society can permit total freedom," "Fidel Castro has enslaved the Cuban people," "America can win in Vietnam," "Communism is an inherently evil and domineering system," "The United States must totally disarm, destroy all its war machines and commit itself to peace," "Capitalism is an inherently evil and repressive system," "American imperialism and corporate diplomacy must be destroyed to protect the Third World peoples," "All power to the People," "Love it or leave it," "Does a government exist to perpetuate itself or to be kept or disposed of by the People?," "Should America pay for external 'security' at any price or reorder its priorities to prevent our internal security from being destroyed by urban blight and ecological poisoning?," or "Hitler had some good ideas, but blah, blah, etc." What I'm trying to say is that the group would have to conduct a self-review to see where each person's head is at and then take it from there.

"Communication games" would be a real test of the viability of the group and their own ingenuity: Communication between the "groupers" is artificially impeded in some way (just as there are barriers in our society between people that aren't real; for instance, if you're black or Puerto Rican you're suddenly "one of them," you're different and though we might talk we can't communicate, or you look like a crew-cut fascist to me, or you're old, or talk with a Southern drawl or for gawd's sake you're a hippy and I can't make somebody like you understand) and to achieve the goals of the group the impediments have to be overcome, put aside or obliterated. I won't go into all the ways that barriers can be created, partly because there are so many ways, partly because the group would have to see what

200   OUR TIME IS NOW

works for them and mainly because you might think up things yourself if I don't cloud your minds with my ideas.

Group expression through films (which would be shown to student audiences) and tapes, as well as fiction and semi-fiction in the form of short stories, plays, etc., trips, whatever kind and to whatever world, musical expression, group involvement in activist causes, arrangements for speakers or rock groups for the Student population, rallies, publications, whatever, experimental projects (*communal living?*, *Student business co-op?*, *think tanks?*, *who knows*), god zeus's, there just ain't no limit to what can be done once people are organized.

So if you're still here . . .

The biggest problem we'll have is fitting the program into time schedules after and during school, so we're gonna have to have the schedules of everyone who is interested and what sort or hours they are free. *We need* about *fifteen Students* for two pilot programs. *We hope* that even if you're skeptical or think *Smuff* is a dirty rag or think I'm a dirty rag or you lean heavily to the "right" —no matter where your head is at—we hope you'll be with us, we need you to work with us, not for *Smuff* or us, but to prove something, to let *them* know that Students aren't mindless, unimaginative, plastic robots who have to be led around by teachers to produce, to learn.

We're not running an exclusive club for "leftists," "pinkos," or seniors, just Students. Whatever, whoever, wherever you are get behind us and support yourselves by telling us you want to be in the program. It can't fall on its face if you don't want it to.

Starting the second you read this we are collecting names and schedules. You can give the stuff to me or Smuffer Edd or you can send it on a nice cheap postcard (or voice questions, criticism or whatever) to: [address given].

My homeroom's room 307, so you might find me there before school.

Just this once prove that you're not apathetic—you'll make or break student power.

The one thought I have to add to Steve's is this: If the students do prove to be too immature to get much out of independent study, whose fault is it? The students should have been given more responsibility long ago; they should have been encouraged to enjoy learning on their own long ago. If they are too immature after eleven years of formal education, doesn't that emphasize the need for freer, more independent study at an earlier grade?

These aren't only *Smuff* ideas, and the students in Hackensack aren't the only ones to try out their own educational programs. The Youth for Peace, Freedom, and Justice in Royal Oak, Michigan, have their own school, Freedom School. They had been criticizing high school curriculum for a time, and finally, they decided to initiate their own alternative.

FREEDOM SCHOOL

THINK!
Vol. I, No. 5
Royal Oak,
Michigan

When the power structure requires more mathematicians, the school system creates more mathematicians. When the power structure requires more mechanics, the school system creates more mechanics. When the power structure requires more middle-class businessmen, the school system creates more middle-class businessmen. Insomuch as we have a compulsory school assembly line, most people turn out conditioned properly.

Youth for Peace, Freedom, and Justice feel that the world requires more free thinkers. We also feel that students should have a free choice in what they learn. YPFJ is sponsoring an alternative to the established "educational" institution. We're sponsoring (for the second and not the last time) a freedom school in which nine courses are offered. The decisions as to whether or not to attend and as to which classes to attend are left entirely to the discretion of the individual.

The courses are:
Foreign Policy
White Racism and Black Power
Myths in American History
Civil Liberties
The New Morality
The Draft
The American Indian
China
Student Power and the American School System

Refreshments will be served. Please attend.

SEMINAR ON RACISM

Racism is the greatest problem in America today. Our white racist attitude displays itself in the crises of our cities, in our foreign policy, and the teachings of our schools. To educate ourselves and others about the nature and depth of racism in our so-

THINK!
Vol. I, No. 1
Royal Oak,
Michigan

ciety, Youth for Peace, Freedom, and Justice is sponsoring a *Seminar on Racism.*

The seminar will be a nine week program of intensive study. It will consist of weekly discussions with experts in the field of anti-racism and outside readings. The topics covered will include: "The History of Slavery," "Institutional Racism," "Racism in Our Foreign Policy," and others.

All people of high school and college age are encouraged to attend the *Seminar on Racism.* It is held every Sunday evening at 7:30 PM at Shrine High School, 3500 W. Thirteen Mile Rd., just west of Woodward Ave., in Royal Oak.

The seminar began on Sunday, April 21, with an introduction titled "Racism, What is It?" This Sunday, April 28, the topic will be, "African History and Slavery." It is not necessary to have attended the first session to participate in the seminar. You are welcome to attend anytime.

For adults who are interested in such a program as *Seminar on Racism,* the Royal Oak Human Relations Council holds a similar seminar every Sunday at 3:00 PM.

For information on this seminar, contact Father Jim Francek at 547–1818.

Curriculum is an area where a lot of reform is called for by the underground. The main criticism is of irrelevant courses. Too many courses are tailored to deal with the world as it was ten years ago, and too many teachers refuse to relate the subject matter to today. A wide variety of courses is offered, but not the right ones. Courses in music appreciation are offered at most schools, but how many schools offer courses in rock music? The curriculum in high schools today has virtually ignored the culture of the students it is educating. Rock is having a tremendous effect on the life-styles of young people in the world today; it is communicating to them. Yet many teachers will insist that it is not a serious kind of music, not one to be studied.

Actually, I have not seen enough underground papers touch upon this area of curriculum reform. While I am sure most students would agree with me that curriculum should be related more to the youth culture, the subject has been neglected except by implication.

What is touched upon more often is the obvious irrelevance of the curriculum to the black community. The banning of *Soul on Ice*, by Eldridge Cleaver, from San Francisco high schools is an explicit example.

Here are two articles that deal with curriculum:

ATTENTION ALL TEACHERS!

We recommend that all biology teachers read the last chapter in the BSCS biology text. It explains that in one year, you (the students) will have forgotten about 85 per cent of the facts you learned in biology and that the purpose of the course was not to have you memorize facts, but to put you in a frame of thinking, in this case scientific.

The authors assume that if you don't go into science, you won't have much use for all the details, but that becoming a person more aware of yourself and environment will make you more easily adaptable to and com-

*MINE
No. 8
Tucson,
Arizona*

fortable in your surroundings. We wish that the course was taught on this assumption, as we wish all required courses were.

It is evident that a forced feeding of facts leads only to the forgetting of them, not to the making of a better student, or a better community, or a better world. In this age of specialization, though electives should be taught for job training, with whatever means necessary, required courses, after providing the basics necessary to life, should be a broadening influence, allowing the student to develop his own patterns of thought. School, therefore, should be a place where in addition to being trained for performing the techniques necessary for earning money, a student is allowed to become a better person in all facets of his future life. Making a living is not restricted to the accumulating of monetary wealth, but includes searching for and achieving wisdom—understanding self and environment, i.e., others—and happiness.

It is then necessary to condemn the school in which the student is removed from the accumulating of wisdom and is not allowed to discover how to achieve happiness. Such a school is only a temple to pre-twentieth century rigamarole.

J. S. Catalina

When the administration of a high school makes a reform, the underground will usually be the first to recognize their accomplishment. This is because the students in the underground are constantly looking for reform. And sometimes the underground can use these reforms as examples to prove a point they have been making for a long time.

GIVEN A CHANCE
Bob Klein

THE OBSERVED
Vol. I, No. 4
Flushing,
New York

A course entitled English 8x9x is offered in our school for the first time this term. This course requires two periods a day, yields two major credits, and is satisfying a long felt want of many of John Bowne's seniors.

What makes this course so different is that with the extra time we can do not only the required curriculum, but also whatever voluntary and in depth work we wish to carry on in class. We can do additional work either as one class or in seminar groups of five to fifteen people. The work done in these seminars is chosen by the students with suggestions offered by the teachers as to what ends each group should try to attain in its subject of interest.

Students in our school have demanded for some time the right to choose their own curriculum. In this class we are finally able to do that. Groups have studied Kafka, Pinter, Malcolm X, Carrol, and others already, and will soon reorganize themselves to start on a new series of topics and authors.

Some people are critical of students on the basis that students want rights, but are unwilling to accept responsibilities. I believe that this course disproves the misconceptions. Students in the class have given their own money to purchase extra books, spent time (not required) out of school for group work and for extra research. The teachers needn't check our homework because they know it has been done and done with interest.

Interest is the crux of the matter. A student can sit

in a class all term, hand in homework each day and walk away with a mark, but without interest, will learn nothing and retain even less. If, as in this class, he can study those things of interest to him personally, he will enjoy doing so.

Given a chance, given the materials, given the encouragement we need, courses like this can help us, as students, to learn and love it.

ROXANA DEVELOPMENT PROGRAM

COMMON SENSE
Vol. I, No. 2
Alton, Illinois

On March 11, 1966, the Roxana School Board approved and gave their blessing to the Development Program that was initiated at Roxana about three years ago. The program, which covers the fields of math, English, and social studies, is to be highly commended.

To qualify for participation in the program, a student must rank in the upper one fourth or one half of his class and must have at least a B average in the particular field he chooses to study. The participants in this program are intelligent young adults who have a desire to think and work; yet the program met bitter complaints which were voiced by an apparently confused group of people. Immediately two questions were raised: Why were these people in opposition to the program? Why was there confusion over such a commendable system— a system which is needed.

The answer, it seems, is that much of the confusion stemmed from a lack of knowledge about the program. This was particularly true in the math division. The parents were not really sure what was being taught. However, after the parents were shown what the program consisted of, the majority were in favor of the program. A consensus was reached among the students, parents, and administrators.

Yet there was still disagreement in the community. This time it came from the "elite" right wing groups. They were complaining that the program was a lot of "propaganda hodge-podge," and that it could give the students the "wrong idea about the American way of government." It is true this program didn't teach that Presidents Roosevelt and Eisenhower were Communists, and it is true it taught the idea that the U.N. was founded to promote peace, but is this "hodge-podge"?

Because the program did not follow the right wing standards, it could be harmful to the youth's mind. In which case would the student be better off—following the right wing philosophy or looking at it intelligently and objectively?

The people of Roxana are fortunate to have this program in their school. They are given a chance to study the American system of government from all aspects. The students are given a chance to really think for themselves.

The students, parents, and administration should stand up and defend this program and not turn into docile sheep and succumb to the right wing tactics.

The Development Program is a major step forward in the process of education and it would be for the good of all if the other schools were to follow in the path Roxana has blazed.

The grading system is a major part of the educational system that many students would like to see reformed. Students argue that grades are like a whip held over the head of the student. They discourage learning for the sake of learning and increase students' hatred of school. Here are some opinions:

GRADES, BAH, HUMBUG!

THE OPEN
DOOR
*Milwaukee,
Wisconsin*

Grades operate in a number of disguised ways. First they are the teacher's equivalent of the caveman's club. Since students need acceptable grades for the desirable scholarships, jobs, and consequent social and economic prestige, the teacher's grading power is a penalty strong enough to give him the final voice in deciding the purpose, content, and arrangement of instruction materials.

Teachers who favor this procedure of dictating usually state that it is a means of "transmitting a traditional body of knowledge." However, they fail to realize that a dictated selection of questions and information results in indoctrination of certain values. They come to think "these are important questions to ask and this is the 'correct' way to answer them." When students are forced constantly to conform in their ideas to those of the system, they are conditioned into uninterested obedience rather than responsible decision making, and they are prevented from becoming questioning, searching, resolving persons.

Secondly, this system seeks to measure in terms of grades those qualities which cannot be measured in these terms. Limiting educational material to what can be measured in grades eliminates from the classroom such goals as the development of ability to know one's self, to enter into serious, mindbending conversation, to think independently, to relate knowledge to obligation, and so on—all of which are necessary for responsible decision making.

On the other hand, by pretending to measure the immeasurable (many teachers, for example, try to rate the value of student effort when they make out grades), the teachers, through grades, can falsely reduce all experience to a search for facts.

Thirdly, grades teach students to compete against each other. Anyone who may attempt to justify such competition may say that it motivates and prepares students for the big competitive outside world. If grades do motivate, then they reinforce a value system that makes equal the acceptability of self with performing better than others. Further, it states the belief that private rewards should and do come at the expense of the well-being of others. The logical outcome of such a value system is precisely the war mentality of the "big competitive world" with self-interest groups pitted rifle barrel to rifle barrel. Furthermore, if one accepts at all the idea that educational process is primarily to create a society of emotionally stable and fulfilled persons, then competition is apparently nonsense. There are simply no grounds for comparing the development of myself with the development of anyone else. Then not only is this competition nonsense, but obstruction. For as psychologists like Abraham Maslow have pointed out, self-realization occurs primarily through human relationships based on trust and acceptance rather than on fear and power struggle.

Thus, since grades teach students to compete with each other for power, status, and rewards, they obstruct self-realization. The grading structure, then, by encouraging competition, confirms operating for self-interest and individual power over peers.

Fourthly, students who have been passive for twelve years in the face of established authority will be superbly fitted for colleges that are based on submission to authority, research production, and scholarly pecking orders. They fit very well into an economic system based on submission to bureaucratic organization, mass production and cutthroat economic self-interest.

This argument against grades is by no means an argument against evaluation. Evaluation, that is, for and largely by the students. If students, their thought enriched by class discussion and reading, are enabled to arrive at standards of measurement personally meaningful to them, if they can avail themselves of the teacher's orally given insights into their personal progress in an area, if they are in a position to choose what to pursue in light of their progress and interests, then evaluation educates rather than indoctrinates.

TERROR-TEACHING FAILS
David Garvin

THE FORUM
Vol. I, No. 5
Paramus,
New Jersey

The "quiz, test, exam, report card-syndrome" simply isn't working. Based on numerous non-functioning and valueless principles of education, this system is to a great extent responsible for the disenchantment of today's students with the present methods by which they receive an education.

The basic fallacy of the system stems from the misconception of many educators that students should (indeed, must) be periodically tested on their progress in a particular course. Otherwise, one can not expect students to learn the material. What has given rise to this situation?

Aristotle has said, "All men by nature desire to know." Yet since the first most teachers have taken the opposite approach, assuming that students have no interest or desire to learn much of anything. Hence, they felt that quizzes, tests, and exams (all tools of the so-called technique of "terror-teaching") were virtual necessities to ensure that students would learn the material. Education solely for the joy of learning became almost non-existent. Through years of conditioning, students, too, have come to accept the "quiz, test, exam syndrome" of education, although it is of little benefit in true education and learning. Thus much of the studying for exams or tests is by nature "cramming." Knowledge gained in this manner is often forgotten within the short span of but two or three weeks.

Another anachronistic concept of our present educational system is marks. How can one say objectively that John's comprehension of the Civil War is worth 93 per cent, while Mary's is only worth 73 per cent? The idea of grading, then, is practically meaningless to the student. Yet he *must* perform well, even in courses which seem to him to be completely irrelevant. Why is this? In order that he get into college, of course! Marks are now being considered more of a "means to an end" in our increasingly college-oriented society. By themselves, they mean very little.

PASS-FAIL

Dear Editor,

I consider myself an average student with an average ranging from about 80 to 88. My question is: What is 80? In school, the teachers mark you in numbers. Should this be done? When I learn what I am supposed to learn, I am usually satisfied. I can't see why I should have to be dissatisfied just because some teacher doesn't like me or doesn't think I've lived up to my abilities.

THE OPEN DOOR
Vol. I, No. 3
Milwaukee,
Wisconsin

After all, the question is: Have I learned what I was supposed to? Not: How much of everything have I learned? Or: How much of this book have I learned? I think that we should be marked on a pass-fail basis. In other words, we are marked on a report card either P or F. I realize that this would be "unfair" to the ones with very high averages, but what of it? It would eliminate the bitter struggle going on between the normal guys and the brains. It would eliminate the brownie system in which teachers (not all of them) mark some guys highly because they get along well. It would, also, give a student more time to learn a course he is actually interested in or will do him more good than another required course. I propose that schools would start with marking required courses this way and gradually proceed to change the others over a period of semesters until all courses were marked this way. This would avoid confusion but still get it done.

Generally (New York is the biggest exception), students in the underground side with the teachers. Although the students criticize teaching methods, they have most of their conflicts of opinion with the administration.

The Gilded Bare, a paper that concerns itself mostly with educational reform, has complained about how low teachers' salaries are probably even more than teachers have.

PRICE OF TEACHING
P. Reynolds

The U.S. Census Bureau statistics show the average salary of an eleventh grade dropout to be $7,392 per year, compared to the average U.A. teacher's salary of $7,330 annually.

THE GILDED BARE
Vol. I, No. 2
Columbus, Ohio

U.A. cannot hope to maintain its quality of teachers with salaries at that level. A number of Ohio cities have pay scales much higher while others are raising theirs in the near future. In order to continue attracting excellent instructors we must remain competitive.

Few people realize that the starting salary for a new teacher with a bachelor's degree and no experience remains at $5,950, which after taxes would leave roughly $4,641. Mr. Richard Canfield pointed out that there has not only been a continued sharp rise in the cost of living, but all signs indicate its continuance. Secondly, male teachers are at present choosing work in industry rather than in education because they cannot afford the salary difference. We must attract men into the profession who will make teaching their career. In this light present pay scales are grossly inadequate.

On Wednesday, April 16, the U.A. Educational Association started negotiations with the Board of Education. Columbus teachers, in all probability, will receive at least a $700 raise this year resulting in pay scales much higher than in Arlington. Therefore, it is imperative to the future of this system that the teachers be supported in their plea for higher salaries.

If your parents should complain that their taxes are too high already it should be stated that not only does

Ohio have the lowest tax rate in the nation, but is fiftieth out of the fifty states in aid to education.

We are fully aware that pay is not the sole issue in attracting new teachers, but present salaries cannot by any stretch of the imagination be considered an added inducement to teach at Arlington.

The Gilded Bare will support the teachers in their salary demands and urges students to inform themselves and their parents of the issues involved.

In *Smuff*, we called for more communication between the students and the administration, something we, and the state board of education, felt was lacking. Putting this article in *Smuff* showed me a lack of seriousness with which the administration listened to *Smuff* requests. I had hoped that the administration would at least comment on what I thought was a reasonable request. But they didn't. Of course, their lack of comment could have been part of their decision to turn their backs on *Smuff*.

Anyway, here is the editorial.

WHERE DO WE AIR GRIEVANCES???
(*Editorial*)

SMUFF
Vol. I, No. 2
Hackensack,
New Jersey
In the middle of last March, the New Jersey State Department of Education issued a ruling that all high schools in the state must form channels for students to air their grievances. The Depart-

ment of Education was aware of general student unrest throughout the country. And they knew that New Jersey high schools are too large for students to express their opinions to the administration effectively.

The high schools' reports about their efforts to give students such means of communication with the administration were due April 1. When the state received the reports, the State Commissioner of Education, Carl L. Marburger, criticized the high schools' plans, saying that they were far too general to be effective. Mr. Marburger then called for workshops this summer to form new plans. He said that he wants more student participation in forming these plans.

But the biggest problem with the plans is that the students don't even know about them. Robert Vare, a reporter for *The Record* who wrote an article about disorder in Bergen County high schools, said, "Not one of the students whom I spoke with had even heard of any such channel."

Hackensack High School is supposed to have a channel for student grievances. Where is it? If there is one, what good is it if the student body is not aware of it? At this point, the only way students can freely express their complaints and criticisms is through *Smuff*. The administration can hardly take credit for that.

The *Smuff* staff respectfully requests that the administration make the students aware of any plan that has been devised. To make sure that a maximum number of students become aware of their new voice, we suggest that a student make the announcement over the public address system. This announcement is far more important than announcements telling whose cars have to be moved from the school parking lot.

So there are some concrete, specific proposals and alternatives. But before I finish the chapter, I would like to give you a larger, more general picture of what some students in the high school underground think a school should be like.

The best example I could find was a result of the teachers' strike in New York. While the teachers struck, parents, non-striking teachers, and students opened the schools to give the students a rather informal formal education until the end of the strike. Stuyvesant, an ordinarily all-boy school, was among the opened schools. The excitement of opening the school, the fact that the students weren't required to be there, the confusion and the informality of the classes all added up to an atmosphere that made learning fun.

STUYVESANT OPEN DURING STRIKE!

NEW YORK HERALD TRIBUNE
Vol. 2, *No.* 2
New York

During the third teachers' strike, classes have been held inside the Stuyvesant H.S. building every school day since Thursday, October 17, with the exception of Friday, the 18th, when the school was locked by the custodian.

On Oct. 17 two classes were held from 9:30 until 11:30. There were three teachers and seventy-one students present.

Friday, the custodian participated in an unofficial city-wide custodial sympathy strike.

On Sunday afternoon, during a Typographer's Union meeting, two fathers and their neighbor entered the building and stayed overnight. When they were discovered in the morning, the custodian told them that he was on their side and would leave them alone. They opened the 16th street entrance at 8:50, where a few students were waiting. They proceeded through the empty halls, to the 15th street entrance, where they opened the six doors, to the shock and apparent anger of the police. As students rushed the doors, the officers pushed as many boys back out as they could. Those students outside understood immediately that they could get in on 16th street.

While the seventy-five boys were settling in the auditorium supervised by two teachers, some seventy-odd Washington Irving girls, accompanied by about twenty teachers, entered through the 16th street doors.

Makeshift classes were assembled in English, World History, American History, and Math until noon, when an assembly was scheduled. At these assemblies, continued every day, anyone was allowed to say anything that was on their mind.

Tuesday morning, the custodian opened the building for Mr. Simon, and the students and teachers from both schools entered. There was a slight increase in attendance. Dr. Fliedner and Mr. Wortman and a Parents Association (PA) representative observed classes. Classes were also scheduled in Physics, Chemistry and Gym. The dietician and lunchroom staff also were in school and prepared lunch at noon.

Wednesday, with attendance still on the rise, an afternoon program of electives was devised, offering classes in Art, Music, Swahili, Political Science, Philosophy, Afro-History, and Poetry.

Thursday and Friday were "normal" school days with attendance around 200, and a City Councilman observing Friday morning. The students held a soul-party in the gym Friday afternoon.

There was a Parents Association meeting on Tuesday, October 22, originally for the purpose of orientation of new students and their parents. Needless to say, there were a great many parents there that wanted to discuss the strike and tell the other parents that school was open and classes were being held. There were also students present who were not permitted to speak by Mr. Sendor (PA President) and Dr. Fliedner (Stuyvesant's Principal). The meeting came to an end at about 10 p.m.

Then, on Friday the 25th, College Night was held. This annual event gives juniors, seniors, and their parents the opportunity to attend lectures on various colleges by representatives from those colleges. There were striking teachers distributing UFT leaflets of the advertisements in the newspapers, and students and parents distributing four various open-school leaflets. One of these contained the actual program of classes for the Stuyvesantians. There were a good many vocal fights outside and a great deal of calm discussion inside.

WE INTERRUPT THIS NEWS ARTICLE TO GIVE YOU A COMMENT ON THE SCHOOL ITSELF DURING THE TEACHERS' STRIKE.

The school was, first of all, some kind of co-ed. There *were* girls. Morning classes, however, were segregated by sex. We were grouped together at assemblies, lunch and during the electives in the afternoon. The girls were a pleasant touch and made school seem more real. The manners that so many boys left outside surfaced as doors were held, voices lowered, and remarkably enough, the jamming and crowding at the front of the lunchline disappeared. Some of the boys were acting, however, as if they hadn't seen a girl since junior high. They gathered, oblivious to the obviousness of the tactic, around the most attractive girls, offering them things that Stuyvesantians hold dear—cake, and forks, napkins and orange juice, ravioli and cookies, etc.

The teachers from Irving were mostly young and

lively. Discussions were commonplace, in the classrooms, as opposed to lectures and classwork. The pressures were gone because we knew that if we didn't want to come, we didn't have to. Instead of discussing a particular book, the class discussed the author, the era, and the theme of the book as one entity. No chapter-by-chapter analysis, those things of the past. In History, the Renaissance was called what it really was, a world-wide Revolution on all fronts. There's not much you can do about Math, but at least the homework was light and not compulsory.

All around school, you got the feeling that maybe this was what education was really about.

Sunday night, at a meeting of concerned parents, teachers, and students from both Washington Irving and Stuyvesant, a fourteen-member steering committee was set up to handle problems as they come up in this present crisis.

Monday morning, school opened as usual, with a tremendous increase in attendance of Stuyvesant boys. The crowds were too big in some classes so that second classes in many subjects were scheduled by teachers with free periods.

At Hunter, classes were held during the strike in the building. Hunter is under the board of Higher Education and the teachers, apparently, are not UFT members. Some girls have been noted as feeling sympathy for the students who were not learning while others have simply felt left out of a special extended summer vacation.

At Brooklyn Tech, classes have not been held. The building has remained locked and whatever feeble attempts were made at opening the building failed. The students have counterpicketed daily against the UFT strike outside school.

As I said before, the underground is people educating each other. They are educating each other to things that are relevant to their lives—their culture.

The youth culture consists of a lot more than students asking for educational reform (not that that is a small

---

EIGHT

Youth Culture: the Rock Revolution

---

thing). And as the underground will be the first to admit, it consists of more than the high school underground movement.

First, there are the *signs* of cultural revolution. Long hair is one. Probably more significant, and definitely more threatening, drug use is culturally acceptable to youth. Sex is treated more openly and honestly by this generation. And rock music serves as, among other things, a means of communication that is peculiar to the young.

Although it is superficial, long hair has played an important part in both the youth culture and the high school underground. For one thing, it was the cause of dress-code controversies and some of the earliest student unrest in the high schools. I was told to get a haircut or not participate in graduation ceremonies in the ninth grade, and the next year I was thrown out of school to get a haircut. Both experiences occurred long before I'd ever thought about a high school underground movement, but the experiences surely had an effect on my future dealings with the administration. And there's more to hair than the fact that it upsets many high school administrators. For the youth culture, it is an expression of freedom to let your hair grow—that you aren't chained to society's rules. Politically, it is often interpreted as a sign of opposition to the establishment. All these symbols may be nice, but most people I know who wear their hair long wear it that way because they like it that way.

Often associated with long hair is the use of drugs. Actually, you don't have to take drugs if you wear long hair, nor do you have to have long hair if you take drugs. Nevertheless, drugs are a significant part of the youth culture. High school health films call drugs an escape from reality. But marijuana, the drug that is most commonly used in high schools, is smoked more socially among young people than as a means of escape. It's analogous to a martini at a cocktail party, although the experience is quite different, and I think that it is easier for someone my age to turn down a joint than it is for his parents to turn down a martini at a cocktail party.

Sex is also sometimes called part of the youth culture. But it is not. At least, not exclusively. The youth culture does, however, have a different *attitude* toward sex than does the culture of our parents. Obviously, we didn't invent promiscuity, but we do seem to be able to discuss sex more frankly than the last generation. This is part the frankness of our generation. In HIPS, for example, a serious discussion and description of birth-control methods was printed, not for sensationalism, but for genuine information.

Probably the most important of the signs of the youth culture is rock music. Peter Townshend of The Who, a well-known rock group, once said that rock music has had more effect on the world in its comparatively few years of existence than jazz had in twenty years. He wasn't trying to put down jazz, he was just saying something about rock.

Rock is communicating to youth. It belongs to youth. It is part of their revolutionary culture.

Rock is not revolutionary because of its history. In fact, it can and has been called a product of the exploitation of blues. Admittedly, Elvis Presley and the Beatles are millionaires because of the capitalist system. Because of this, it seems ironic when the underground criticizes capitalist exploitation of rock.

Personally, I don't put down capitalism. However, I do see what the underground is objecting to.

A few years ago, a lot of San Francisco groups, Jefferson Airplane for instance, started playing for free on the streets. It was a great thing—a real part of the youth culture. The music they played, "acid rock," was having a great effect on the culture. Drugs were being used very heavily at that time, and young people were finding out a lot of things about themselves. "Dropping out" was the big thing, and it was an important part of the evolution of the culture. Later, most young people decided that "dropping out" wasn't the way. But still, they valued the freedom of the music then. The idea that this music that was moving along with their culture belonged entirely to them, not even partly to any capitalist businessman, meant a lot to them. Forget the history: now, this was entirely their music. Can you blame them for objecting when the music started to be exploited again?

Rock music and the youth culture are stronger today than ever. Woodstock showed America just how massive the culture is. Hundreds of thousands of young people, a large percentage of them still in high school, came together not for something political, not for something underground, but for each to do what he wanted and yet remain in a gigantic community. It was the music that made them a community; it was the music that they came to hear.

Politics, of course, is an important part of the culture, but right now rock is moving generally away from politics. You don't have to be politically aware to be part of the youth culture, just as you don't have to take drugs to be part of it. I would certainly never divorce rock from politics completely. I don't think anyone can do that. (The MC5 is an example of a rock group that is very political.) However, as the author of the following article says, you don't have to be politically aware to like rock.

MUSIC
Jon Gottlieb

A REBIRTH OF
WONDER
No. 3
New York

You don't have to be radical to love rock music; it doesn't even help. Most of the record-buying kids of today are about as aware as eggplants. As a matter of fact, it was the switch from Folk to electric that virtually ended "protest" songs. If rock was not such a high-paying industry, this deradicalization might not have occurred. Artists tend to lose some of their revolutionary fervor when they sign a contract of $500,000. Would you finance the revolution if somebody gave you $500,000?

It is foolish to talk about the revolutionary power of the music industry. The performers have less prestige than anyone. They are bought and sold like has-been baseball players. The power that exists is not revolutionary because it is in the hands of the record company owners. These men decide who gets the $500,000 contract, and you know that if a group is "dangerous" they won't be the ones moving to Beverly Hills. And even if they are, by the time they get to Beverly Hills, they've turned into the very people they used to condemn.

A tangible power structure is required if you want a really peachy revolution. You can't write home about a bloodless coup without swallowing your pride. There is no real power structure in music, so there is nothing to overthrow. It is hard to be oppressed in a mansion; this proves very embarrassing for groups like the Fugs and the MC5 because their music is based on shock value alone, and in the music world, no one is shocked for very long. Barry McGuire never had a follow-up to "Eve of Destruction," but the Ohio Express will keep baking saccharin cookies like "Yummy, Yummy" and "Chewy, Chewy" until we all need our stomachs pumped.

What it comes down to is that political music and political art in general are very negative. Most people would rather listen to "positive" music like Traffic or Buffalo Springfield or "mystical" music such as that of Bob Dylan than to "negative" music (MC5, etc.). The imagery of Procol Harum is eminently more satisfying than "Kick Out the Jams, Motherfuckers."

In my previous statements, I have tried to make clear my feeling that it is ineffective to criticize society from the vantage point of Columbia Records. Musicians are generally apolitical or apathetic. Many famous figures in rock have rejected politics completely. In "My Back Pages," Dylan uses his special style of imagery to express the same point of view the Beatles state in "Revolution." Both express a definite distaste for movements that try to change society as a whole. "You tell me it's the institution, you better Free your mind instead!"

My revolutionary friends say that no one is Free unless everyone is Free. Most artists feel they can transcend or "rise above" the false political world. It is a question of communities. Artists consider themselves a separate community, exclusive, inclusive, and, except for material needs, self-sufficient. Revolutionaries, as a rule, try to be a part of the working class community. A person totally involved in his own creative work is always changing. Music is in a state of constant evolution. An artist's world moves very quickly and is never the same two days in a row. A functioning artist is not exposed to the feelings of stagnation that bring on revolutionary attitudes.

I find myself resting uncomfortably between both communities. I cannot advocate killing, but I also cannot ignore the injustices of the capitalist system. The reason I cannot be a total revolutionary is that I feel there is no system in which these institutions do not exist in one form or another. Government is Government; structure is structure is structure; bureaucracy is bureaucracy; and capitalism is communism with one more letter.

While most rock groups do not give political messages to their listeners, still some groups perform songs that call for action. Unlike the Barry McGuire-type protest songs, these songs are not a long list of complaints against society; they are a screaming voice for revolution.

The MC5 is this kind of group. The official group for the White Panthers (a white radical organization), the MC5 performs political music that shocks some people. Here is one high school underground writer's description of the effect the MC5 in concert had on Cincinnati.

KICK OUT THE JAMS
Rick Starr

Saturday, June 28, marked a revelation in music for this area. This was the night the MC5, the most controversial group to hit the public, played at the Black Dome.

IN-BETWEEN
Vol. I, No. 8
Hamilton, Ohio

Prior to Saturday, the Dome was in trouble—if the Saturday show hadn't drawn a large enough crowd, it would have closed. But all attendance records were broken as approximately 1,500 people were crammed into the Dome.

This inevitably caused problems. The MC5 could not play on the stage because they had too much equipment, so they played on the floor, cramming the crowd almost beyond the breaking point. Temperatures up to 135° were recorded. The show was still worth the suffering as the MC5 put on the best show the area has seen, comparable to Hendrix, the Grateful Dead, and Jefferson Airplane concerts. The group itself had no individual talent, but put together they were pure hell.

Someone once said the MC5's type of music was "guerrilla rock." This was proven doubly over as the five hypnotized the crowd with songs like "I'm Sick to my Guts of the American Ruse," "The Human Being Lawn Mower," and, of course, "Kick Out the Jams" twice.

All of a sudden it's realized what is needed to get a message across. Instead of saying, "Why don't we love each other and dispose of the jams together," came the cry, "Godammit, kick out the jams, you mothers!" This is why the MC5 are so popular—they don't mince around when they have something to say. This was also the case for such greats as Lenny Bruce, Zappa and the Mothers, and the Fugs. They all realize that in order to be different, to get what they want heard, the crowd has to be shocked into listening. The MC5 certainly said it all Saturday. Cincinnati may never recover.

Most rock groups do not give political messages; nevertheless, they communicate.

And the underground papers talk about them. The *New York Herald Tribune*, for example, devotes much of its space to rock, because its editor, Toby Mamis, sees rock as "one of the prime means of communication and change for youth." Sometimes the articles discuss what's going on in the rock scene. Other times they review specific albums or concert halls. Anyhow, both types of articles are evidence that rock is important to the youth culture.

BOOGIE
Marvin Schwinder

THE GLASS
EYE
Vol. I, No. 3
Teaneck,
New Jersey

I just have to turn all of you on to the Boogie. Canned Heat's Refried Boogie (Living the Blues on Liberty Records)—all forty-one minutes of it— is the ultimate rock experience. Recorded live, this dish captures much of the excitement of a hard rock concert.

OUR TIME IS NOW

The boogie is one of the most basic of blues beats. It envelops your body and mind (depending of course, upon your mind). You'll be missing plenty if you miss the boogie.

The solos on this recording are tremendous. First, Al Wilson, the rhythm guitarist, displays his mastery of complex chord progressions. His finger-picking is precise—sometimes he plays three melodies at once.

The bass, played by Larry (Mole) Taylor, is simply the best electric bass solo yet recorded. On this ten-minute solo, Taylor proves that he can produce it better than most lead guitarists. He can play better, faster, and more complex music.

The exception is Henry Vistine, the lead guitarist. He is able to develop one theme, the boogie, into a solo embracing jazz, rock, and the psychedelic technique. After many minutes of fast picking and note bending with the group providing background, he is left to his own. He ascends a stairway of one climax after another, and it goes on and on. When the band returns, Henry Vistine breaks into another round of piercing music. It seems to me that most guitarists' hands would be quivering in contorted motions, but Henry Vistine plays on and on.

It seems very difficult to top that, but Fito de La Pena, the Heat's drummer, just about manages. He plays the fastest rolls and the most complex rhythms in rock. During his solo, you'd swear you were hearing two or three drummers, but it's all Fito. He plays sans sticks, everything! His playing alone is worth the price of this fine double album.

Bob Hite, the leader of the group, does the vocals. He has a unique voice, partially because it is very earthy, and partially because Bob Hite is a very hairy, almost primitive, person. He is wild, and he makes you do the boogie, and you'll be glad you did.

Everybody must do the boogie.

MONTEREY POP
Toby Mamis

WEAKLY
READER
No. 11
New York

A year and a half ago, Jon Phillips (Mamas and Papas) and Lou Adler organized the first (and last) Monterey Pop Festival. The TV rights were sold to ABC-TV, but when they saw the film, they decided that they didn't want it. So now it is ready for theater distribution as "Monterey Pop," by D. Z. Pennedaker.

I can see why ABC didn't want it. Filmed in documentary style, it is technically poor. Pennedaker and his chief assistant, Richard Leacock, were both, at one time or another, students of Jean-Luc Godard. The camera work is often unsteady and rarely more than what the screamingest teenybopper would do with a zoom lens as a toy.

I hate to use cliches, but, here goes. This film is good, if only as a history of rock in one of its better moments. For those of the viewing public that don't get to concerts too often, there are lots of good parts to it. For all those Hendrix and Joplin worshippers out there, it will be good listening. And for those of us that dig Otis to any great extent, it makes one feel religious to see him in action. Also, those of you that missed Big Brother's tour, this is your last chance to see the group in action. Don't stay away from this movie, but don't pay too much to see it, either. The Jimi Hendrix excerpt is one of the finest in the film, a portrayal of one of his first American concerts after returning from England a success. He does all the usual obscene things to his guitar, including burning it and sexually attacking it. It reminds one that *everyone*

232   OUR TIME IS NOW

in rock and roll, it seems, has learned a great deal from Pete Townshend and The Who, who also appear in one of the better parts of the film.

RECORD REVIEWS
Terry Patten

The Notorious Byrd Brothers, The Byrds, Columbia.

THE MESSIAH
Vol. I, No. 3
Lombardi, Illinois

The Byrds have long been one of the most creative groups in America. With each of their new releases, they have participated in the exploration of a new musical frontier. Their reputation as great musicians is well deserved. From *Mr. Tambourine Man* to *Younger than Yesterday,* their melodies, arrangements, vocals and musicianship were excellent. Then two members of the group left and the remaining trio released *The Notorious Byrd Brothers.* The unmistakable style of the Byrds remains. The electronic effects are more pronounced and the composition and performance are adequate. Unfortunately, the whole effect is just that, adequate. The music is not of low quality, but it isn't of high quality either. The Byrds have evidently become *too* mature. The music is not really exciting in the way that "Eight Miles High" was. And it isn't as well written as "Turn, Turn, Turn."

Listening to this album was, for me, a very depressing experience. It points up the fact that the Byrds as well as many other once great groups are over the hill. If you are a Byrds fan, you will probably like this record. If you don't sense anything wrong, though, listen to "Get to You," which is undoubtedly one of the worst written songs that I have ever heard. With so much really exciting new music being produced, I don't understand why you would want to spend your money on this. But at least it is better than spending your money supporting the extortionists who profit from the sales of Monkee records.

THE ELECTRIC CIRCUS
Toby Mamis

NEW YORK HERALD TRIBUNE No. 5

THE NEW ELECTRIC CIRCUS OPENS AMIDST RICH PEOPLE AT A BENEFIT FOR THE URBAN CO-ALITION!!

I had occasion to visit the NEW Electric Circus a couple of times during Easter week. If any of you wondered how they could make it any worse than before, see for yourself. It is smaller, uglier, hotter, and greasier. You now enter a black-lite lobby, walk past the always crowded checkroom, up a regular staircase, into a large white cavern. That is the dance area, with a self-contained area off to the side and up a few stairs where one can see the whole idiotic scene. There is also a stage for the performers, and a staircase up to the tier, where there are holes in the wall to climb in, and windows from which you can also see the whole dance floor. Pablo's light show is also upstairs. Once safely in the downstairs section again one can buy an unusually expensive Pepsi, and go into the ROOM. The ROOM is a dark cave with a merry-go-round in the middle, with six compartments, that each fit two or three people. All around the walls, there are places to sit, with two little sunken pits (perfect for two) in each of the farthest corners. Then there are the rest rooms. Don't miss them. The price is still steep, and the sound system is still good. I saw Elephant's Memory, Cat Mother and the All-Night Newsboys, and Sly and the Family Stone. Catch the latter two, and forget the first. After midnight, when all the old people left, the crowd loosened up, and there was a lot more friendliness.

Now a trio (Jesse Colin Young, Joe Bauer, and Banana), they are almost a new group. They have a different sound—one that moves in a very Tim Hardin-like direction (especially in vocal style). Young's bass work is more than adequate, and Banana's guitar is the best it's ever been. They've been living in San Francisco, which helps, I'd venture to guess. The publicity release that accompanied the album I received in the mail has a line that goes like this:

"Capped a two month concert tour of East Coast colleges at the end of 1968 with a sell-out performance at N.Y.'s Fillmore East."

They were the third attraction on the bill; the audience was there to see Iron Butterfly and Canned Heat. The Youngbloods were the highlight of the show for me and a few other people, but the publicity statement is only slightly misleading. But better that you should believe RCA, and buy the album, because they rate it. It isn't very often that RCA comes out with a winner, but this is one.

Two RCA products that are not winners are FRIENDSOUND, a fake experimental record (featuring some ex-Raiders who used to be with Paul Revere), and THE FRIENDS OF DISTINCTION, but they're no friends of mine. A super-slick soul group, with an orchestra behind them. Of course they're black, and the liner notes are by Jim Brown.

The underground press does not try to convince its readers to smoke marijuana. But since marijuana is part of the youth culture, papers will sometimes encourage its readers who do smoke to spread the seed. (You don't have to smoke marijuana to read or even edit an underground paper; it doesn't even help.)

JOHNNY POTSEED
Larry Siegal

SANSCU-
LOTTES
No. 30
New York

There comes a time in the life of every self-detesting pothead when he scrapes the bottom of his stash with his feverish fingernails and finds nothing. This is when he becomes, quite literally, down in the dumps, sifting through the ashtrays, scraping the plastic of his pipe stems and smoking it as "resins." (Oh, fire and brimstone, what a tragedy!) But let us see if he has really done everything possible for his head. Generally, in his all-consuming search around his room, he uncovers one or two pot seeds. Angrily, he steps on them or kicks them under the bed. Everybody knows there's no value in smoking seeds. But, wait a minute. There's such a thing as biology. Enter the humble pot seed in a new light—Hail Mari, Father of Pot.

Aside from the obvious advantage of not having to pay for it, there is a special reason at the present time for growing your own—*The Berkeley Barb* recently reported that U.S. planes have been dropping defoliants on the pot fields of Mexico! (Oh, those dastardly fiends!) Gather together friends—we have a mission— to foil the defoliants.

Planting the seeds is no problem. Find a not-too-obvious place (not your backyard or fire escape) with possibly a great many tall weeds to hide the weeds in. Plant the seeds anywhere from 1½ to 5 feet apart, possibly throwing a few in each hole to insure a good plant in each place. Some people suggest soaking the seeds and leaving them in wet tissue paper for several days to help them germinate. Plant somewhere around ¾ of an inch deep, and wait. The best areas for pot planting are cool and dry or hot and humid. The soil should be rich but not swampy, since young plants get uptight when they're submerged. Very, very important is to have a great deal of sunlight.

There is sex in the pot world, but you'll be able to tell all about that when the flowers appear, generally about eighty days after planting. The male will have wide greenish-yellow or purple flowers with five (count 'em five) stamens. The females will have small stemless flowers, which frequently crown together and appear like a spade. The female, in general, is the one that will turn you on (wouldn't you know it) but take the male too; what the hell, the worst you get is low-grade catnip.

The time when the amount of resin is the largest is when the flowers appear, but if you want to do the whole gig over again, wait a couple of weeks for the seeds to start falling and then just turn the soil over them. At this point, you have a choice between simply breaking the stems near the ground or digging out the roots. The latter when the roots are stuck (with the rest of the plant) into boiling water is called "curing"; add sugar and you've got sugar curing.

The problem is now to dry the plants. The best way is with a sunlamp, which requires only two days; failing that, simply hang the plants upside down for about a week. Drying in ovens is controversial, since some claim it evaporates some of the cannibis, and some say it makes it stronger. If you can inhale whatever leaves the oven when you open it, you're safe either way.

It only remains then to mangle the plant into such a shape as to fit your pipe, and try it out.

Pot growing can be a very rewarding experience: twenty-five pounds of marijuana have been claimed from a single plant. At the very least you should get a few ounces. It can also be dangerous—the cops, for some reason, are very much against it. The plant does not look very much different from an ordinary weed, so only the fact that a "long-haired creep" is constantly walking over to a particular plant, sniffing it, fondling it, will tip the fuzz off. The plant only needs regular watering and attention until it is solidly settled in the ground —be cool with that and then stay away from them as much as possible. So, scatter your seeds to the wind, we'll have this country on its ass yet.

Media are very important to this generation, the first generation to be bombarded by television for its entire lifetime.

Radio stations, especially FM, express the youth culture. Stations such as WNEW-FM in New York are honest in their expressions of the culture. They play young people's music without censoring it, unlike many AM stations.

The AM stations that pretend to be serving youth are the target of criticism by the underground. People involved with the underground usually see this as another example of capitalist businessmen exploiting their culture.

Television programs that deal with the youth culture are also criticized. Programs like the "Mod Squad" that I suppose are meant to appeal to youth are often looked at as weak attempts at brain-washing. They may be trying to appeal to the youth culture, but the only thing that television and AM radio are accomplishing is the alienation of many young people—and sending them to FM.

WNEW-FM: A NEW VOICE IS HEARD
Lenny Lubart

THE FORUM
Vol. I, No. 5
Paramus,
New Jersey

To speak of WNEW-FM is to speak of the leading proponent of progressive rock music in this area, if not in the entire country. The station bills itself as the "new groove" and this self-assessment is indeed accurate. Songs played on WNEW-FM may often not be heard on any other radio station in this area. Arlo Guthrie's "Alice's Restaurant," a twenty-five-minute song, is but one number that is heard only on WNEW-FM. Another favorable aspect of the station is that the complete version of all songs (such as "Light My Fire"—Doors) is played, rather than the cut version heard on AM radio.

The star attraction of WNEW-FM is Rosko. Rosko, a disc-jockey, is like none other. Before coming to WNEW, he worked for numerous other stations, notably WOR-FM. When Rosko first commenced working at WOR, he was given a substantial amount of freedom in the selection of records to be played. Shortly thereafter, however, executives of the station began pushing only the best-selling and most popular songs. Rosko could not accept this restricting policy and he soon resigned. Several months later, he signed with wnew-fm. Having questioned general manager George Duncan as to how much liberty he could have, he was asked, "How much do you want?" Rosko's response was, "You've just given me all I need."

Rosko devotes part of his show every evening to poetry reading, together with a short "sermon." They can be concerned with almost anything. For example—

"It's going to happen one day . . . when a judge will say to an offender . . . 'You're a free man' . . . and the jury will turn to him and say, 'But we found him guilty' . . . and the judge will say, 'I know that and he knows that . . . he's free of his shackles of bar [jail] but not of his shackles of guilt.' As Dylan just said, '99 years is too much.' "

Coming from Rosko, something like this packs quite an impact.

One of Rosko's favorite expressions is the "mind-excursion" or as it is often called—"the hippest of all trips." These phrases do not refer to LSD "trips," but rather to the concept of "getting stoned on reality." Rosko says, "What I really mean by 'mind-excursion' is to relax, to get away from the falsehoods, and the travesties, the burlesquing of reality. I'm saying when you're off at five o'clock, relax and find *you*. That is the true 'mind-excursion.' "

Rosko's popularity has been on the constant upswing. He can now boast 250,000 listeners a week, second only to wabc. This fact is truly amazing when one realizes that only 50 per cent of the homes in his listening area even have fm radios.

KILL UGLY RADIO
Peter Tonks

MINDFOOD
*Vol. I, No. 3
Pelham,
New York*

You have undoubtedly been subjected to *ugly radio* and heard a "hot new group's" brand new record, which sounds like a carbon copy of the previous record. *Ugly radio* fans either lack the intelligence to detect the absurd similarity often present between the old and new release, or obviously enjoy the insult, which is likely the case.

There are two reasons why many times a new release is identical to its predecessor: (1) A greasy A&R (arranging and recording) man with a beer belly, cigar, and a silvery Klein's Nehru jacket (with medallion) figures that because the group's record sold 93 million copies and got them top billing on "American Bandstand," the follow-up record, to insure its selling, should have the same characteristics of the old one. So he creates a record with the exact same chords, beat, etc. Of course, he relies on a gullible audience, which, needless to say, the American audience is. Consider the "Woman, Woman," "Young Girl," "Lady Willpower" degeneration. All three sound identical; all three were number one on *ugly radio*, and each one makes one throw up faster than the last one. But, obviously, a select group of greasy individuals enjoy and buy this junk, much to the delight of the fat A&R man who collects the teenage money, then grinds out more garbage. (2) The second reason is simply that the group has no talent, so it *can't* produce anything but the crappy Xerox material. If your overtaxed teenage brains will recall that standard of schlock-rock, "Expressway to Your Heart" by some forgotten greaser group. Well, their carbon-copy follow-up, "Explosion," has identical chords, beat, etc., and has the exact same break where the phoney lead singer's syrupy voice drools all over the microphone. However, the most notable case of record duplication belongs to that ever popular group, ? and the Mysterians, who hit the charts way back in the summer of '65 with "96 Tears." (Yes, kids, that *was* the summer "Hanky Panky" replaced "Strangers in the Night" as number one.)

Well, anyway, that group had a piece of shit out last year called "You Captivate Me," which has the *exact* same amateurish organ; only the words to both songs are different.

The duplication of lousy records is only prolonging the sickness that is *ugly radio*. People like William Drake, who owns a chain of top forty stations throughout the country, dictate what is and what isn't to be played. His takeover of the once good wor-fm last year is why that station is today no better than am's *ugly radio*. The phony disc-jockeys play all the carbon-copy trash, actually thinking it is creative material and a change from the last record. "Well, here it is: big number one this week!! 'Lady Willpower!' What a great song! This one goes out to Tony and Debbie, bla, bla, bla, bla, bla, bla . . ."

ARTICLE
Paul Bilsky

THE GLASS
EYE
Vol. I, No. 3
Teaneck,
New Jersey

"Christ, you know it ain't easy. You know how hard it can be. The way things are goin', they're gonna crucify me."

This is the new single record just released by Apple

records by the Beatles, "Ballad to John and Yoko." It has been banned from people by the businessmen who run WMCA and WABC. Undoubtedly, the major reason (if you can call it a reason) behind banning it is the use of the word "Christ" in the chorus.

Friends, this is obscene. Jesus Christ preached love and peace to the world, and to try to silence his name because of this is typical of society—absurd!

Another interesting facet is what the proprietors of WABC have for the grease, and the other for everybody with a little taste. They allow the song on the FM station, showing their hypocrisy. The reasoning behind not banning it on FM is that they would probably lose their listeners.

My opinion of the song itself is that it, as most Beatle work is, is fantastic. I am sure that if it were released without any controversy, it would have outsold their other current single, which is the current AM hit (number, numberrrrrr111). Whether or not these uppity businessmen who exploit teenage gullibility will release the record is yet to be seen. I hope that it will sell and maybe then the AM stations will gain a better insight into what is happening (ohhh groovy . . .).

WANTON BITCHERY
F. B. J.

THE AMERICAN
REVELATION
Vol. I, No. 7
Elgin, Illinois

Mod Squad or HOW TO WASTE AN HOUR ON TUESDAY

The Tee Vee industry has got to be the most retarded industry in the United States. Its pitiful attempts to gauge the mood of the country stop being funny after Monday and get downright sickening by Tuesday. Typical of this mass media mess is *The Mod Squad* (Tuesday, 6:30, ABC). It appears that those responsible for this slop thought they could make modern day Eliot Nesses out of three turncoat narcos. So they have created a monster show about three ex-hip-bikers who go around doing their best for Law'n Order and engaging in such heroic activities as beating the crap out of flower children.

But it just don't come off! *Mod Squad* is the kind of show during which a person forgets the first half hour before the second half is over. The plot is the same cops and robbers stuff that's been blasting at us since we were born (right in front of the Tee Vee). And the characters, they're right out of "beach-surfer" movies and Coca Cola commercials. Add to this some forty year old grade Z script writer's idea of how young "mods" talk and you've got a long haired version of the Hardy Boys (or Spin and Marty if you remember the Mickey Mouse Club) and their Lady Clairol girlfriend, suntanned Nancy Drew. *Mod Squad* is nothing but a phony, tinseled, Madison Avenue version of modern America.

Probably the one person who spoils the youth culture even more than the exploiting capitalist is the phony.

TOM TERRIFIC AND HIS WONDERCOLUMN:
SUNSHINE HIPPY
(*critics*)

THE AMERICAN
REVELATION
Vol. I, No. 4
Elgin, Illinois

Thomas Paine once, while discussing the Revolution, talked of the "sunshine patriots." These were men who were "patriotic" to the rebel cause when it looked as though the rebels were winning. (If the English seemed strongest, they became Tories.)

In today's avant garde revolution of everything Establishment (clothes, politics, mannerisms, goals, et al.) the rebels are known as hippies. There are many persons hip to the rebels' cause mainly because it is the cool, "in" thing to do.

These "in" people speak of love, peace, flowers, brotherhood. They wear flowers, love beads, medallions, and wild beautiful colors. They talk the way *Life* magazine says they should. They listen to psychedelic music. They can be seen every summer on the Strip, in Old Town, the Haight, or the Village.

They read *Time, Look, Life, Post,* and find out what to be like to be cool. In one of the aforementioned publications they read the address of the *East Village Other* or some other psychedelic paper and find out where it's supposed to be at. They can be seen only in the summer.

In the winter they put on the regular clothes, cut their hair to a middle-class long so that it is short all around, but a little hangs down in the front. They forget peace and love. They say, "Shoot the rioters," "Drop the bomb on North Vietnam," "Peace and love are cool, but they aren't practical."

Tom Paine felt contempt toward the "sunshine patriot." He disliked them more than Tories.

Despite its exploitation and despite phonies, the youth culture is strong. So strong that it is feared by certain conservative adults.

"Motorede," a decency organization in Arizona, is an extreme example of a group of adults who fear cultural revolution. They fear rock music and open discussion of sex, specifically, in sex-education courses. The "Motorede" sometimes seems ridiculously paranoid, and this is not that common among adults. But one thing that the "Motorede" people have going for them that most adults don't is that they take the music seriously.

MOTOREDE PROTESTS ROCK!
J. Chamberlain

MINE
No. 8
Tucson,
Arizona On May 5, 1969, at 8:00 p.m., at Amphitheater High School, MOTOREDE (Movement to Restore Decency) sponsored a speech by Dr. Joseph Crow on "Propaganda with a Beat." (Or how American youth are being destroyed and made ready for Communism by rock music.)

The turnout was approximately 25 per cent for Crow, 75 per cent against, with about 100 young people waiting outside who could not get in.

After Dr. Crow gave his life history, he began playing songs and analyzing them. "Itchycoo Park," "Sock It to Me," "Crystal Ship," and others were shown to be pushing drugs and sex.

OUR TIME IS NOW

The reason that youth are so susceptible, and will rush out and use drugs just because they hear about them in a song is, he said, because music soothes and lowers resistance. Also, similar to a Pavlovian theory, the frequent rhythm changes in songs cause youth to slowly become neurotic and more susceptible to propaganda.

Dr. Crow claimed that the plot was obviously instituted by the Communists because of the studies Soviet psychologists have done in the area of brain-washing. The 6,000 American prisoners of war in Korea provided many case studies for the Communists, so they could understand how to better brain-wash American youth.

He cited the satire, "Back in the U.S.S.R." and the growing class consciousness of youth as proof that the Communists were succeeding. "Revolution" was compared to V. I. Lenin's *Left-Wing*.

At the close, Dr. Crow advised those present that at the door one could purchase his packet of materials on how to effectively prevent Communist influences for a mere $1.75.

COMMIES INVADE SEX-EDUCATION PROGRAM IN ARIZONA

"SEX EDUCATION that goes beyond the biological facts of life . . . IS JUST A LITTLE BIT RED."

So says former Republican state senator Ernest Garfield.

MINE
No. 7
Tucson,
Arizona

Before a packed house of *fifteen* people at the Pima County Republican Club, Garfield said that the Communists were behind the effort to establish progressive sex education in Arizona schools.

He also said that the Communists had admitted doing this grisly deed.

Garfield said that several years ago the Commies and other such types said they were going to "rewrite" the textbooks of the U.S. They did this, he said, to corrupt the moral fiber of American youth by taking their minds off the army, church, and other "all-American" type institutions and put their minds on the ugliest, most degrading part of life: sex and family life.

Since Garfield made this particular speech, he has joined and is apparently leading a group of "concerned" parents called "Motorede" (Movement to Restore Decency).

These dirty-minded people have since requested the school board and the state legislature to ban all sex education from Arizona schools. All sex education is part of the Communist-Liberal conspiracy, they claim.

These people who are members of Motorede should first ask themselves these questions: (1) Have they ever had a frank discussion with their children on sex? (2) Are they qualified to explain Venereal Disease? (3) Where might one find one of those "rewritten" textbooks? (4) How did the Communists manage the very difficult task of brain-washing all the sex education teachers in Arizona? (Are the Commies really that smart?)

These are the questions that worried anti-Communists should ask themselves on their lawns at 7 o'clock in the morning.

AN ANSWER TO MRS. MoToReDe
Fred Pascoe

MINE
No. 8
Tucson,
Arizona

In the most recent issue of the SHS newspaper, an article quoted Mrs. Ann DeMeglio as saying, "I see no wrong in a child learning something behind the barn door, as it were, or the haystack. Why is that child behind the haystack? Because he knows that it is something that is secretive; it's something you don't go about broadcasting in a public classroom. That's why he's there, and besides that, how much harm can he do behind the barn door?"

Well, Mrs. DeMeglio, what is this child doing behind the barn door? Is he there because his or her parents haven't had the time or the inner fortitude to tell them where they came from or about sex? Most children do *not* go behind the barn door to talk about sex; they go there to *have* sex. It is not known whether or not you think that the sex education classes practice coitus, and if you do, your protest has good cause. But, if you think that it does less harm to have sex in a barn than to talk about it in a classroom, you have another think coming!

Do you realize that practicing sex in a barn can result in pregnancy for some unfortunate girl or in venereal disease for either? There are also mental aspects to consider. In a sex education class a person learns biological function and structure and healthful attitudes such as the only time people have children under healthful circumstances is when the two people are married, and when the people have a child when they aren't married, serious social mishaps can occur.

I think that sex education is very much needed in today's society because it gives a child an understanding that a parent is unequipped to give.

One of the largest, most violent attacks on the youth culture came last fall in Berkeley, California. The young people were defeated, but since then they, especially the high school underground, have shown that they are ready to fight to keep their culture. Or take it back if it is taken from them.

The attack was particularly significant to my way of thinking, since it wasn't an attack based on capitalistic values but was an attack filled with senseless violence. And this violence made it one of the worst attacks our culture has felt.

BERKELEY PARK PROTEST
Bruce Woodworth

SMUFF
Vol. I, No. 2
Hackensack,
New Jersey
There's an old lot in Berkeley, California, owned by the University of California. It wasn't cared for, and over the years had become a dirty mess, used by no one.

Some local young people and Berkeley students received a constructive idea several months ago. They cleaned it up, and made a happy park for happy people. Grass was planted (the legal kind). They went to the mountains and brought back young trees and ferns. Vegetables were planted. Swings were provided for the little children, and for those who are young at heart.

Several weeks ago, suddenly, in the middle of the

OUR TIME IS NOW

night, bulldozers were brought in. By morning, when it was too late, all that had been created was utterly gone. A dirty lot was there again, but now it was surrounded by a fence, with signs ordering everyone to "keep out."

It had been called "People's Park," named by the people who created it. They have decided that it will not die like this. Protests and demonstrations were organized and hundreds of angry young people clashed with the police. Violence erupted and guardsmen with fixed bayonets helped the police with their clubs to disperse the masses of young people. James Rector, 25, was killed by the police. A National Guard Helicopter sprayed tear gas on the campus, choking everyone; teachers, students, and protesters alike. The faculty at the University of California was appalled. Fifteen hundred professors protested the police actions. Strikes were called and teachers refused to hold classes. About thirty faculty members led a parade of two thousand amid handclapping and shouts of "We want the park." Math professor John Kelly said they're trying to determine ". . . whether the university has acted dishonestly and stupidly, or just stupidly."

People's Park is still fenced, but the fight goes on, and one day it may grow again. But James Rector is gone forever.

TAKE BACK WHAT'S OURS!
SUPPORT BERKELEY

The people of Berkeley, California, built a park on a vacant lot. They called it "PEOPLE'S PARK." The rulers of California took it away last week.

FLYER
New York

YOUTH CULTURE: THE ROCK REVOLUTION   251

Their cops had to club, gas, and shoot its defenders . . . one was killed, one was blinded, and over 100 were shot. Whenever we build something, whenever we create something—they move into our space!

This weekend, at the Coliseum, the corporations' showcase for their products (cars, boats, cameras, etc.), "American Youth" will be put on sale. "The Teen-age World's Fair" is free Pepsi Cola to make us believe that to be part of the "Now Generation," we have to buy their crap. It's fashion shows of clothing manufacturers telling us that expensive bell bottoms make us hip. It's Columbia telling us that our music costs $4.50 a record and that concerts are at least $2.50.

Our music belongs to us—at least it should. It's ours —we created it—we played it—but the record companies are making us pay for what is already ours. And except for a few that "make it," the musicians get screwed.

A Columbia record advertisement reads: "The man can't bust our music." But Columbia (cbs) is the man and he already has.

We can have long hair and talk differently as long as we are part of the consumer society. We can even be stoned as long as we pay to hear concerts and buy their plastic psychedelic shit. The Berkeley people made their own music in their own outdoor concert hall. They took the ideas of our music seriously. They were building a revolutionary community—a threat to the Establishment. That's why the cops came, that's why the National Guard came, that's why shotguns were fired into the crowd, and that's why James Rector, 26 years old, is dead.

OUR CULTURE IS OURS! COME TO THE TEEN FAIR TO TAKE IT BACK! Memorial Day, May 30th—New York Coliseum—7:00 PM—West 59th St and Broadway
High School Student Union—information 799–2020

The high school underground press is only reflecting the youth culture when it talks about drugs, sex, and rock. The writing itself is a reflection of the culture. The flavor and content of the articles both express young people.

Here is an article that isn't political and doesn't talk about the youth culture. But it expresses the ideas of a young person.

BATHROOMS

You know the bathrooms in this place are kind of funny. At least they are for me. Every time I go into the bathroom I get bombarded with all the different niceties that go into the construction of a public restroom. The main thing you feel is the unflushed toilets. Then there is always the large variety of smokes. There is always cigarette smoke; that's the heaviest one, I mean the one that hits you the hardest. Then every once in a while you'll go to a restroom of distinguished people and smell pipe tobacco, but it's always either cherry or maple. I remember I once walked into this john where this guy was smoking cherry pipe tobacco. I was really scared he would chase me out so I left. There are all these other smells that go into the recipe for the public bathroom. But everybody smells

INSTITU-
TIONAL
GREEN
New York

them. That's not what makes bathrooms different to me. When I walk into the bathrooms in this place I get very strong memory waves. You know what I mean. It's like the feeling you get when you hear an old song you remember real well. Some people think I'm a little kooky, and when I told them that I get these memories in a bathroom they thought I was really insane; that's why I haven't told anybody in a long time. This will probably be the last time I'm telling anybody so I might as well tell the whole thing. I mean I might as well say what they remind me of; it's kind of silly.

When I was about twelve, I went on a long bus trip. There were all these kids on the bus; I guess we were all about twelve. Anyway, a couple of kids were making out. I wasn't, I was talking to the guy next to me. I wanted to talk to him because he was the pitcher on the baseball team and a kind of important guy to know. So anyway I was talking to this guy when this girl comes over to me and sits on my lap. She interrupts the whole conversation by saying something real retarded, so me and this pitcher stop talking, so it's just him looking out the window and me sitting in the aisle seat with this girl on my lap. She starts acting real retarded. She started doing all this stuff like touching my nose. She must have learned it from the lady on Walt Disney. Well anyway she did this stuff like touching my nose and rubbing my chin for a long time. Then she looks around the bus at all the kids making out and says, just like the Walt Disney lady, "You wanna make out?" Now I'm no square and I know that it's pretty good when somebody wants you to make out with them, so I said okay. She bent over and kissed me on the right side of my lips. Man, did she have bad breath.

Well, that's what the bathrooms in this school remind me of. Don't tell me I'm a kook, because I'll be sorry I told you.

Paul Steiner, the "fiery editor-in-chief" of *Sansculottes* (now defunct), wrote an article for HIPS and the *High School Free Press* last year that sums up much of the meaning of the high school underground and the youth culture and their relationship to each other.

Steiner, who has been with the high school underground for a long time (I believe he started as a freshman), writes with rhetoric that is directed to youth. In this article, "High School Liberation Front," he intends to communicate to youth. When he says "everybody hates school," he does not mean it literally. And when he uses the word "work," he is defining work as anything that you don't want to do. (Obviously, using the conventional definition of work, Steiner himself is a hard worker. He was editor of a sixteen-page publication that came out regularly. But he enjoyed this, so he would call it "fun.") However, when Steiner uses the word "revolution," he means it.

The quotes that are included in paragraph one come from the lyrics of "(I can't get no) Satisfaction," written by Mick Jagger and Keith Richards.

Here it is:

H.S. LIBERATION FRONT
Paul Steiner

NEW YORK
HIGH SCHOOL
FREE PRESS
No. 6
New York

NOWnownownownownownownow
NOWNOWNOWNOWNOWNOWNOW

"the truth is what is; what should be is a dirty lie"
—lenny bruce

"to live outside the law you must be honest"—bob dylan

"if your children ever found out how lame you really are, they'd kill you in your sleep"—frank zappa

This society does not allow us to satisfy our desires. "Baby better come back maybe next week." We are forced into a daily battle against the repression of our lives. "When I'm watching my TV and the man comes on and tells me how white my shirt's to be." Society requires submission to consumption and alienation. "He can't be a man 'cause he doesn't smoke the same cigarettes as me. I can't get no . . ."

In high school, we have to constantly deal with deans, administrators, and authoritarian teachers. The structure of the school, with the power appointed from above, and the structure of each class, with the words of the teacher equaling the truth, serve the purpose of training students to accept the present system and their places in it. What matters in school is that you stop questioning and criticizing and begin to memorize what you're told is right. It makes no difference what it is (math or social studies) or whether it's true (black people were happier in slavery), what you dig by the time you get to high school is to give the right answers on the test.

And it doesn't really make any difference because the

256   OUR TIME IS NOW

class doesn't mean anything to your life anyhow. What's worse than giving answers you know are wrong is that you have to go to classes in geometry when you don't give two shits about the area of a triangle. The point of high school is that you learn to accept doing things which are meaningless to you so that you can achieve some other goal, like college or a job. And you don't really want college or the job either, but you need them so you can achieve another goal—money. And you don't *need* very much money to live, you just need it for things which you've been taught to want. Food, shelter, clothing, and love can be had for free, but that's another rap.

What is necessary is to find out for yourself what your real needs and desires are. Not intellectually by studying a whole bunch of dead philosophers, or at least not just by intellectual reasoning, but by doing what makes you feel good. That's what we want to change society into anyhow, a place where people can do what they feel like without being repressed or starved. The hang-up that a lot of people have is that they work for that kind of change. Working for a cause does the same thing to your head as working for a boss. You do things you don't want to do. After a while, you can no longer deal with your life except after-hours. If we are to build a new society it must be as we destroy this one. If we separate the two we'll just build new bureaucracies and new rulers after we destroy the present ones.

And as long as we have hierarchies and leader-oriented organization we are not going to change anything. We must develop a type of organization that can fight what's going down and at the same time begin to realize the joy of the present moment.

Affinity groups came out of the July 4th riots on Telegraph Avenue in Berkeley. It happens naturally— when the cops charge, you stick with your friends. You learn to act as a unit when attacked from the outside— ties of love, politics, friendship, and survival make each group fast, effective, together. You start living/acting as a group. Your needs are satisfied within the collective. Your fight for survival is based on your commune: Attacking the repressive society around you is an act of self-defense. Hostilities are directed out. You become an integral part of an organ, not an organization. Demonstrations are planned as the need arises. They are no longer demonstrations, they are life/theater. In a group of five to ten, everyone is a leader. The distinction between your individual needs and the external demand for revolution breaks down.

Affinity groups can never completely work until this society is destroyed. We are all fragmented people because we have been shaped by what exists and the dreams of fragmented people are obstacles in the road of revolt. Our groups must be open to change and must constantly search for something better. Enough rhetoric, the thing is to build affinity groups in the high schools.

An important thing to get straight is that affinity groups are not The Vanguard, waiting for the right moment to lead the Masses in revolt: They are the revolt. If certain things are your rights—the right to cut, to smoke in the bathroom, to wear pants, to learn what you want to learn, then don't wait for the administration to grant them. Take what belongs to you. If it is your right then it cannot be granted: Rights are yours from birth. If you stop making excuses to deans and teacher aides they freak out because their basis is that you believe what you're doing is wrong. If you refuse to recognize their authority, they are forced to use the only power they have—pig power. And the more they use this power, the more students will refuse to accept their authority.

Groups begin to take on different functions. With a used electric mimeo (about 120 bucks) you can pour out a constant communication of where you're at and what's happening. Doing something, then writing it up, running it off, and giving it out in school combines action, theory, creation, organizing, education, and learning how to work/play within the group and the school as a whole. By your example of action and your communication of its meaning you create and spread a sort of liberation front. Those who were not directly involved in the action are touched by your newspaper/poster/leaflet. The important thing is to cause a reaction. Bringing people out of the deadly school apathy doldrums. Make people face their real emotions. Whether they accept or reject you is not the issue, they have been forced to react on a gut level and the more that happens the harder it is to program them into our computerized alienated society. Everybody hates school, relatively few understand why there is nothing wrong with hating it.

The left has generally had little to offer except Utopian ideals of the future. Now we have a whole way of life that rejects plastic America by its presence. We have rock music, underground newspapers, long hair, dope, beautiful clothes, joy, sex, a hip community, and revolution. Say it loud, I'm hip and proud. We have to break down people's barriers against having a good time. Society teaches us that fun is sinful and work is saintly. Bullshit, the work/study/get ahead rap is used to keep us in chains.

We've got to start exploring our real needs with other people who are hip to what's going down. We've had TV's, cars, and subscriptions to *Life* magazine. It's time we started subscribing to life. It's time we started relating to our friends without the sterility of society's rules. Once we have begun to define our own reality we have, at the same moment, declared war on the official reality of school and the system.

Go out and do it. The revolution is now!

The high school underground movement has already had a great effect on high school students throughout the country. For many students, the underground constitutes a more important part of their education than does their school. However, this underground will not last forever. Eventually (hopefully), the

Postscript And It's Just the Beginning

student activities/learning experiences that have been initiated by the underground will become established parts of the school systems. This, of course, is a goal of the underground. Surely some of the excitement of the underground will be lost, but it will be well worth this small loss to have schools that provide better, more relevant learning experiences.

Anyway, this is a long way off yet. The underground is still in its early stages of development. And as it continues to develop, you will see it take new forms. In my school, as well as in many others, some of these new forms have already begun to develop. The independent study course that was discussed in Chapter 7 is one of these forms. *Smuff* is already branching out into new fields of education. Another form will be the *Smuff* film festival that was mentioned in Chapter 4. We have already ordered underground films to show and are planning panel discussions after the films. One development that I haven't mentioned is that Edd Luwish, the present editor of *Smuff*, took a course last summer and in now a qualified draft counselor. *Smuff* is also working in 1969 to get the New Jersey eighteen-year-old vote referendum passed.

In New York, Toby Mamis, editor of the *New York Herald Tribune,* is starting his own school with about twenty other students. They will formulate their own curriculum and teach each other as well as get occasional outside lecturers. Non-accredited, Toby's school may be the ultimate in underground education.

Will Toby's school illustrate what the high school of the future will be like? I can't say and neither can Toby. He won't really know what it will be like until it is started.

Then what *will* the high school of the future be like? Different. It will surely be freer; students will be more independent. High school students of today haven't reached any peak of possible maturity. The students of tomorrow will be more mature than we are. We were never doing organizing in junior high school. Joshua Mamis (Toby's younger brother) is. And he'll be in high school in a few years. Just as administrations have already become more liberal about dress codes, so tomorrow they will become more liberal about studies. And "formal education" will become less formal.

Besides all this, my generation will be growing up and taking over positions in teaching and administration. We may mellow with age, but I am certain that we will still change the school system to a greater extent than most people would suspect.

And as the schools change, so will society.

Of course, all this is speculation on my part, and in case you haven't gathered by now, I am not God. But one thing I can say with certainty. This is only the beginning.